Preaching Radical and Orthodox

Dedicated to the memory of John Hughes,
who began this project

Preaching Radical and Orthodox

Sermons for the Christian Year

Edited by

Alison Milbank, John Hughes and
Arabella Milbank

scm press

First published in 2017 by SCM Press
Editorial office
3rd Floor, Invicta House,
108–114 Golden Lane,
London EC1Y 0TG

SCM Press is an imprint of Hymns Ancient & Modern Ltd (a registered
charity)
13A Hellesdon Park Road, Norwich,
Norfolk, NR6 5DR, UK

www.scmpress.co.uk

British Library Cataloguing in Publication data

A catalogue record for this book is available
from the British Library

9780334056416

Printed and bound in Great Britain by
CPI Group (UK) Ltd

Contents

III. Unfolding the Story: Lent to Easter Sunday

IV. Real Resurrection: Eastertide to Trinity Sunday

V. For the Time Being: Trinity Season and Christian Lives

Saint Mary Magdalene Preaching
c. 1500–1520
John G. Johnson Collection, 1917

Contributors

Silvianne Aspray (née Bürki) is a minister of the Reformed Church of Switzerland completing her doctorate at Cambridge on sixteenth-century metaphysics and Peter Martyr Vermigli.

Dr Anthony D. Baker is Clinton S. Quin Professor of Systematic Theology at Episcopal Seminary of the South West, Austin, Texas.

Jeffrey P. Bishop is Professor of Philosophy and holds the Tenet Endowed Chair in Health Care Ethics at Saint Louis University. He is also a former priest in the Episcopal Church.

Dr Ian Boxall is Associate Professor of New Testament at the Catholic University of America, Washington, DC and parishioner of St Joseph's, Capitol Hill.

The Revd Dr Matthew Bullimore is Vice-Principal of Westcott House, Cambridge.

The Revd Dr Robert Chapman is Vicar of St Thomas the Apostle, Hanwell, West London and Post Ordination Tutor on Liturgy and Mission.

The Right Revd Stephen Conway is Bishop of Ely.

The Revd Dr Andrew Davison is the Starbridge Lecturer in Theology and Natural Sciences at the University of Cambridge.

Kirsten Pinto Gfroerer is pastoral associate at St Margaret's Anglican Church, Winnipeg, Manitoba, Canada.

The Revd Rachel Greene has served as Chaplain of Trinity College, Cambridge, Associate Priest of University Church of St Mary the Virgin, Oxford and Curate of the Benefice of Sturminster Newton, Hinton St Mary and Lydlinch.

The Revd Canon Dr Peter Groves is incumbent of St Mary Magdalen, Oxford and Senior Research Fellow at Worcester College.

Stanley Hauerwas is Gilbert T. Rowe Professor Emeritus at Duke Divinity School and a communicant at the Church of the Holy Family in Chapel Hill, NC

The Revd Dr John Hughes served his title in the Parish of St David with St Michael & All Angels, Exeter and was Dean and Chaplain of Jesus College Cambridge until his early death in 2014.

The Right Revd Dr John Inge is Bishop of Worcester.

Dr Ruth Jackson is Research Fellow at CRASSH (Project on the Bible and Antiquity in 19th-Century Culture).

Fr Fergus Kerr, OP is a theologian and editor of *New Blackfriars*.

Dr Simone Kotva is Junior Research Fellow at Emmanuel College, Cambridge and Affiliated Lecturer in Philosophical Theology in the Cambridge Faculty of Divinity.

The Revd Dr Philip Krinks is Assistant Curate, St Faith's and East Winchester, and Research Associate, Centre for Theology & Community.

The Revd Dr Melanie Marshall is Chaplain of Lincoln College,

Oxford and served her title at St Michael and All Angels, Bedford Park, London.

The Revd Anna Matthews is incumbent of St Bene't's, Cambridge and Ely Diocesan Director of Ordinands in the Diocese of Ely.

The Revd Canon Dr Alison Milbank is Canon Theologian at Southwell Minster and Associate Professor of Literature and Theology at the University of Nottingham.

Arabella Milbank is an ordinand in Lincoln Diocese, currently studying at Westcott House.

John Milbank is Professor Emeritus of Religion, Politics and Ethics at the University of Nottingham.

The Revd Dr Jeremy Morris is Master of Trinity Hall, Cambridge, and was formerly Dean of King's College, Cambridge.

The Revd Prebendary Dr David Moss retired from being Principal of the South West Ministry Course in 2009.

The Revd Dr David Neaum is Chaplain and Fellow of St Catharine's College, Cambridge. He has served in parishes in Cambridge and Dorset, and at the University Church of St Mary the Virgin in Oxford.

The Revd Canon Dr Edmund Newey is Sub Dean of Christ Church, Oxford and has served in parishes in Manchester, Newmarket and, most recently, Birmingham as Vicar of St Andrew's, Handsworth and Area Dean.

The Revd Professor Michael Northcott is Professor of Ethics at the University of Edinburgh and an Episcopal priest who also assists at the Church of Scotland parish of Durisdeer.

The Revd Canon Professor Simon Oliver is Van Mildert Professor of Divinity, Durham University and Canon Residentiary, Durham Cathedral.

The Right Revd Dr Nigel Peyton is Bishop of Brechin in the Scottish Episcopal Church.

Dr Jeff Phillips is Tutor in Philosophy and Theology, Westcott House, Cambridge and Director of Studies in Philosophy at St Edmund's College.

Catherine Pickstock is Professor of Metaphysics and Poetics, University of Cambridge and worships at Little St Mary's Church, Cambridge.

The Revd Dr Gregory Platten is incumbent of All Saints, Friern Barnet.

The Right Revd Dr Stephen Platten is Hon. Assistant Bishop of the dioceses of London, Southwark and Newcastle, and Chaplain at St Martin-within-Ludgate.

The Revd James Robinson is Assistant Curate at St Wulfram's, Grantham and St John the Evangelist, Manthorpe.

The Revd Richard Stanton is Assistant Curate, The Assumption of the Blessed Virgin Mary, Attleborough, Norfolk.

The Revd Dr Jenn Strawbridge is Associate Professor of New Testament Studies, University of Oxford and Caird Fellow in Theology at Mansfield College.

Fr Joseph Vnuk, OP is President of Catholic Theological Institute, Port Moresby, Papua New Guinea.

The Very Revd Dr Frances Ward is Dean of St Edmundsbury.

The Revd Canon Professor Graham Ward is Regius Professor of Divinity at the University of Oxford.

The Right Revd Dr Martin Warner is Bishop of Chichester.

The Revd Dr David Widdicombe is Rector of St Margaret's Anglican Church, Winnipeg, Manitoba, Canada.

Introduction

Go to my brothers and say to them that I am ascending to my father and your Father, to my God and your God. (John 20.17)

We have chosen as the patroness of preaching that is both radical and orthodox the 'apostle to the apostles', Mary Magdalene. As the first person sent out by Christ himself to proclaim his risen life, she has a claim to be the first preacher of the gospel. In the frontispiece image, taken from an early sixteenth-century altarpiece of her life, Mary is preaching, as legend had it, to the inhabitants of Marseilles. She stands, thoughtful and relaxed, as gentle as she is authoritative, with her right hand in one position of the orator in classical tradition, her left hand opening her body's compassionate and pregnant s-curve. This hand steadies her pose by resting on the pulpit nature lends her, a triangle formed by three trees, imaging her participation within the life of the Trinity, in whose name she speaks as a Christian evangelist. So our Mary is an image of the act of orthodox proclamation, the announcing of the Word from within the life of the Church, which dwells in 'right praise', as orthodoxy can be translated. Orthodoxy here is not a limit to expel, but an invitation for all to join the Trinitarian circling life of love given and received. So the grouping of the listeners forms a further triangle around her, with the point at the intersection of the dresses of the women in the foreground. A third triangle leads the viewer's eye down through Mary's gaze to the face of the Marian grouping of the mother and child, and across to the older woman in worldly scarlet, whose upturned face returns us to Mary's hand, raised to preach and to bless.

Preaching also draws us to the foot of the cross, to Calvary, the other signification of the three trees, to find there the love and pardon that will turn our lives around. The word 'radical' comes from the Latin, *radix*, root, and Mary, rooted within her arboreal pulpit, is primarily radical in that her preaching is from the Root himself: it has the authority of one who knew Christ, encountered the risen Christ, and was told to take the good news of Christ to the disciples. Mary also preaches through herself, the example of a life changed by Christ; in preaching, she seeks to move others as she herself has been moved. Hence her orating hand is not stentorian, flung outwards, but cupped towards her own body, where the womb shape made by her drapery suggests how she births the Word through herself. She is a grassroots preacher, proclaiming among the people, barely raised above them on a grassy knoll, her manner authoritative in its gentle concentration alone. In the *Golden Legend*, Mary's preaching was a radical challenge to the reigning gods of the local inhabitants: her prayer in their midst brings idols crashing to the ground. Like John the Baptist, she is a voice of critique crying out in the wilderness: so she preaches *without* the city whose proximity is suggested by the decorous garb of her gathered congregation.

And consequently the word is radically generative, as many of the auditors' responses show, provoking discussion and further teaching, from the turbaned man to her immediate left who instructs his neighbour, to the fascinated gaze of the woman sitting on the right, to the child with his hand on his heart – whose white clothes suggest he might himself be future priest or preacher – and even to the small baby, the apple of sin kept away from him by the hand of his mother, inverting Eve's role in a *topos* often seen in paintings of the Virgin Mother and Christ.

Like Mary, the editors and contributors to this volume of sermons situate themselves joyfully within the creedal Christianity of the universal Church. They look to our common roots in Scripture and the early Church writers as a resourcing of the faith. They want to recall the whole Church to its origins and, paradoxically, this means to a prophetic recovery of what has been forgotten in order to speak to the present authentically. It means challenging the idols of our contemporary world, and offering a transformative vision of experience.

So what is good preaching, radical and orthodox?

First and above all else it is part of divine worship. Indeed, as Pope Emeritus Benedict reminds us, 'it *is* divine worship', just as worship is also proclamation.[1] Good preaching mediates between praise and action, so that our worship is generative and our action the perfection of praise. To merely moralize would be to separate action from the gospel that inspires it; to curtail its lived consequence would be to parody Christ's word. For those whose sermons are gathered in this volume, preaching is a sacramental act that makes something happen: it is performative. To preach is never to be illustrative but to enable a sacramental encounter with Christ himself.

If preaching is part of divine worship, then this means that its form – the manner and style in which we preach – is not a mere tool. The interpretation of Scripture by the People of God is part of the Bible's inspiration, by which it continues to be breathed through by the Spirit. Every word, simile, parallel and joke should accord with our sacred calling as proclaimers of the word and have a decorum, to use the rhetorical term, a fittingness for that proclamation and for those to whom it is to be proclaimed. There will be references to film, art, political events and music old and contemporary – but these are never used uncritically. Like St Paul preaching at the Areopagus in Athens in Acts 17, we interrogate our present-day culture to discern the buried desire for the unknown God, but we judge each cultural artefact or practice in Christian terms. Preaching to unbelievers in today's marketplace, we too must speak from within the space of the Word, collaborating to render it hospitable to others. As far as we can, we do not allow society or politics to dictate our agenda but rather view our own historical moment as a *kairos*, a moment of crisis and decision in which our task as preachers is to uncover the real and salvific opportunity for the revelation of God's purpose for his world. In that sense, preaching is eschatological, a calling to the world to acknowledge the kingship of Christ. This involves an inner tension, an intensification of the ever-present gap between the Word and its acceptance and fulfilment in us.

Radical preaching must therefore be prophetic, and indeed, Hosea, Amos, Jeremiah and all the prophets of the Old Testament are our models, in their clarity of faith and vision, their living in tension with their age, and in their use of symbols and concrete images to communicate God's challenge. It is part of the charism of a radically orthodox sensibility to see clearly the truth that the construction of a discrete secular world is itself an idol that must come down. In our preaching this means that we do not treat any aspect of the world as 'outside', for all is God's and reclaimable.

A third important aspect of the preaching offered in this book is faithfulness to the lectionary and through it to the liturgical year. This is itself a radically orthodox move, reclaiming the galvanizing power of the traditional sacred colorations of the calendar. It is not ourselves we preach but Christ crucified: to avoid the common discipline of the Church in reading Scripture together is to risk privileging a singular, or personal, interpretation of the gospel. It is to shy away from the power of the Word to touch us on the raw. The tension we live is to be found in the relation of Old and New Testament, and our preaching should model a Christian hermeneutics of using love as our interpretive key. 'God is his own interpreter' as William Cowper put it in his hymn, and in Christ we find that illumination that will help us deal with difficult texts. Augustine taught that where a loving and charitable reading could not be sustained, as with the massacres described in the book of Judges for example, one should look to a figurative reading, pointing forward to Christ. This reading through Christ will not sugarcoat or smooth over the violence, but catch it up towards its healing *telos* through the fulfilment held out by the narrative of redemption. We should not avoid such challenges but deal with them, so that we can be equipped missionally to answer those who question the Christian commitment to peace, and that we might encounter and see truly the horror and violence of the present age.

The lectionary is also important because through its overarching narratives over the course of the liturgical year we live in sacred time. We literally follow Christ in his life, ministry and death, as well as following the creation, fall and redemption of the whole world, while we anticipate the End. This is itself a deep fidelity to Scripture, because the Bible as a single book is structured in this way and, by faithful following of the lectionary, we allow holy writ to interrogate us and to find our place in its story. We are gathered as God's people by it, and rescued from the aggressive and deathly self-grounded individualism of our time.

The lectionary and the rhythm of the liturgical year refashion us into people living to God. Radical Orthodoxy, in the narrower sense of the theological tendency of that name (to which many of our contributors would subscribe), has at its heart a theology of participation, in which our goal and purpose as creatures made in God's image is to share in God's life. This means that as creatures we acknowledge our weakness, transience and dependence on God as our Maker; but that very acknowledgement is what makes our sharing in God possible. The Eastern Churches have long had this deification at the heart of their theology and spiritual practice, and the charism of contemporary radically orthodox Christians (to which all our contributors would subscribe) has been to witness to this wonderful truth in the West, also finding this belief in witnesses as diverse as Jonathan Edwards or Thomas Aquinas. There is a dynamic in our participation that is a turning of the whole person: a *metanoia*. As with the Augustine of the *Confessions*, our sense of distance, of alienation from God, opens a desire for union, and propels us into God's arms. Preaching should be a kind of catapult, catalysing this change of heart. Stirring up the soul to believe does not, however, require overblown emotional rhetoric, for the Word itself has its own power if we allow it to breathe through us. Nor, in stressing *metanoia*, should we be masochistic. The action of preaching as part of the liturgical action is to move us from purification through illumination to union with Christ. God's drama – his Divine Comedy – in which we are protagonists takes the tragic wholly seriously while building to the happy ending of the *eschaton*.

The rich arc of the liturgical year offers varied 'moods': encounters with particular paradoxes and themes of Christian experience that are symbiotically blended with the seasons and changes of the year in a providentially given fusion of the natural with the supernatural. Opening each of the five sections of the book are further reflections on how the context of each season shapes its proclamation, interfusing with the individual one of our finite lifespan from birth through to death.

A fourth aspect is the importance of story in preaching. We have already alluded to the way in which listeners can find themselves within the biblical narrative. Our cover painting, however, moves beyond Scripture to legends about Martha, Mary and Lazarus travelling to France to spread the gospel. In the background can be seen the legend of Mary's miraculous rescue of a mother and baby lost at sea, and of her last days as a contemplative in the caves of Provence. The story of Martha's taming of a dragon that had been troubling a town in Provence, whose innocent death at the hands of the townsfolk leads to their naming their town Tarascon after the martyred monster, was given the UNESCO award of 'Masterpiece of Oral and Intangible Inheritance of Humanity' in 2005. The stories of the saints reveal that our own lives have value as sacred story, that they can take on a sacramental quality and become holy legend. Nottinghamshire newspapers reported several stories about Malcolm Jarvis, who died recently, that have this salvific potential. He was an ordinary community policeman, but he once stood up to the legendary football manager Brian Clough for treating a young fan roughly. In the poisonous and violent atmosphere of the 1984–85 Miners' Strike he had dispensed fatherly advice and home-made flapjack to the picketers. These stories exhibit the Christomorphic in protection of the lost and outsider, the avoidance of violence, and forging of peace.

The value of recent stories and ancient legends as generative narratives is something we would seek to reclaim for preaching. We need to embed our hearers in their own Christian culture and tradition, to offer narratives that help us to develop the virtues and to re-imagine our world as poetic and enchanted.

Most of the sermons in this collection are from eucharistic services, where preaching makes us ready to receive the Lord. We call this service the Eucharist because it is a sharing in

Christ's own prayer of thanks to the Father for the gift of himself. Eucharistic preaching not only proclaims the deeds of God from creation through redemption and resurrection; it gives thanks that salvation is achieved: a present reality in our lives as well as an eternal truth. The command to Mary to 'Go ato my brothers' is one that is impelled by gratitude. Mary must stop clinging to the human teacher but see in him the ascended Christ, who will take her with him to 'my father and your father, my God and your God'. Christ offers her a sharing in his divine life. So our preaching, as eucharistic, gives thanks that Christ is truly God and has saved us: and this witness to our salvation demonstrates our understanding of his true humanity. 'God became man so that man might become God' as the patristic adage had it, and in the term 'man' is Adam, man and woman together. If our preaching is to be of any use, it must allow our hearers to see, hear, touch, taste and smell the gospel truth. It must awaken a desire for Paradise as the longing we have all had to be loved, to love and to give thanks. Place, occasion, music, architecture, people and even the weather, all are part of the elements that make a sermon but they must all become Eucharist, thanksgiving, and be offered up as part of Christ's own offering of himself.

Mary Magdalene, conglomerate though she may be of several faithful followers of Jesus, is our pattern here again. She has her jar of precious balm, and she will break it open and offer it to all. So must we, who seek to allow the gospel to speak through our lips, offer ourselves – our imagination, our word-hoard, our mistakes, our experiences, our prayer and experience of Christ – as our oil to pour out in love for Jesus, and for love of his people.

What we have set out in this introduction is a blueprint for a radically orthodox preaching; one with which we hope many who have never even heard of the specific theological movement might concur. It is also a clarion call to continue to proclaim Christ in this way. We are deeply aware that support for what is expressed here goes far beyond those whose sermons are included; space and time have placed a limit. The vitality of a radical orthodoxy in a younger generation has led to the number of sermons included here that were preached in a university context, by and to young people:

this is something we unabashedly celebrate. At the same time this collection does contain suggestive range: contexts of urban deprivation as well as rural establishment; sermons delivered for the young and the not-so-young, for those new to, and for those experienced within, the Church. It aspires to much more for the future.

I

Reclaiming Time: Advent

Preaching as a sacramental act is already a reordering of time, in which the saving acts of God are made present and available to the listener. When the liturgical cycle begins in Advent we start the new life, against the dictates of the secular calendar, in the old year, commencing with this the re-establishment of God's time as our primary medium of experience. A parody of Advent theology awaits reclamation in the already/not yet of secular commercial anticipation: the Christmas Spice latte in late October, and beyond December 25th only a Boxing Day Sale of Judgement when the value of the gift receipts is made all too plain. Unlike the secular version where the tinselled festivity, referring to no higher good or indeed further time, offers as its climax only more of the same, Advent's urgent expectancy works with the natural coloration of time as the year descends into the wild darkness of the December days prior to the solstice.

Advent confronts merely linear time with a complex yet sustaining layering of different but complementary cycles of temporal experience, which Cyril of Jerusalem describes vividly:

> There is a birth from God before the ages,
> And a birth from a virgin at the fullness of time.
> There is a hidden coming, like that of rain on fleece,
> And a coming before all eyes, still in the future.[2]

The believer holds together the awaiting of the incarnate God's arrival at Christmas, the birthing in her own heart like the dew on the fleece given as a sign to Gideon, and the final arrival at the *eschaton*. In the first awaiting, the believers also recapitulate the history of the people of Israel as they look for the promised Saviour. Time and history is narrated as it points to Christ, and we are invited to reach across temporal divisions, and against the economic values given to time, to reclaim our own time's eternal value as part of this story.

The richness of this temporal unfolding is lost when the second coming is underplayed, as so often in contemporary preaching. Only with that final reality can evil be held to account, and our resurrection life be asserted. Only with imminence is immanence realized, Christ's coming as fully historical from Judea to judgement. In the Advent promise, past, present and future offer God to us, and the preacher has to unite them in a proclamation that has John the Baptist and the Virgin Mary as hinges. Like John, we look back to Isaiah and the coming Day of the Lord, and call people to repent; like Mary we reach into that past to find the resources to open ourselves to the salvific horizon.

The important work of Advent preaching, then, is to flow with the richness of the lectionary readings and hymns that inhabit this triple temporality, and offer the paradox of the 'already' and 'not yet' as a temporality that is also gift: where we find all the time we need. It can and must be, especially in this season of the Last Things, truly parousiac – as Henri de Lubac puts it, drawing on patristic tradition: 'preaching is the white horse of the apocalypse', in which the preacher brings his or her auditors to a sense of the crisis of Christ's presence.[3] Our sermons in this section are examples of this offering of temporality as open to the fullness of the *Parousia*, when time will flower from the apparent circles and lines of our experience into the spiralling heavenly rose of Paradise, in which all our lives will be enfolded.

Lifting the Veil on the World

St Stephen's House, Oxford
Revelation 21

Dr Ian Boxall

In Advent we have the privilege of hearing chapter after chapter from the book of Revelation. If Hosanna ('Save indeed!') is the Advent word par excellence, then the Apocalypse of John is the Advent book par excellence. Because perhaps more than any other book in the Bible, John's Revelation is about Advent, about the first Advent of Christ, and about the final Advent, and about those other Advents of Christ in the in-between time as the Church waits expectantly.

So here's an opportunity not to be missed. But before I reflect with you on our reading from Revelation 21, I ought to say a few words about the difficulties of reading this extraordinary book. Reading the Apocalypse requires us to read in a particular way, to see reality more deeply, to view the world more intensely, to lift the veil onto that truer world which is normally just beyond our reach, and can best be hinted at through myth and symbol. So perhaps in this build-up to Christmas, when the alternative worlds of Narnia, Middle-earth and Hogwarts tend to dominate the big screen, and there is a lingering hope that this year might just be the year when we hear sleigh-bells in the sky, and when just occasionally there is the expectation that we might even hear the angels singing, perhaps this is the season of the year where the Apocalypse might open its secrets to us.

In other words, when we listen to the book of Revelation, we are invited to engage our imaginations and see the world through different eyes. It is a capacity that comes more readily to some of us than to others, like William Blake, the English poet, artist and visionary, who wrote that, where most people see a disk of fire when the sun rises in the sky, he saw 'an innumerable company of the Heavenly host crying, "Holy, Holy, Holy, is the Lord God Almighty"'.

Reading the book of Revelation is just such an invitation to see in the rising sun an innumerable company of the Heavenly host. To see terrifying beasts where one expects to see politicians, and angels lurking on the street-corners. Or to see in the figure of a crucified man a mighty Warrior, riding out on a white horse with his vast army of white-robed martyrs. In other words, not simply to engage our brains, but to stretch our imaginations.

At the climax of that kaleidoscope of visions, John sees the ultimate end of our Advent waiting:

> Then I saw a new heaven and a new earth; for the first heaven and the first earth had passed away, and the sea was no more. And I saw the holy city, the new Jerusalem, coming down out of heaven from God, prepared as a bride adorned for her husband (Rev. 21.1–2).

First, the final coming of Christ brings about 'a new heaven and a new earth'. We need to be particularly careful here, because John's vision is regularly read as if what we are waiting for is the total destruction of our old world, including that which we hold dear, those places that we hold dear, even those relationships that we hold dear. The old and familiar, we are told, is so rotten to the core that it needs to be destroyed to make way for a shiny new spiritual replacement. And there are millions of Christians in today's world who think that this is precisely what John does see: God slowly but surely masterminding the countdown towards the earth's nuclear destruction, perhaps with a little help from his earthly friends, and with its crucial last stages played out on a map of the Middle East.

But I want to suggest emphatically that this is not what John sees. A God intent on destroying his creation cannot be the Alpha and the Omega. A God who obliterates the old in favour of a brand-new replacement is not the God 'who makes all things new'. Hence the Fathers have tended to read John's vision quite differently. St Andreas of Caesarea, for example, perhaps the most famous Greek commentator on the Apocalypse, puts it thus: 'it does not mean non-existence of creation but a renewal for the better'.[4] What we are waiting for in Advent is the renewal of that which we know into something even more glorious, rather than its obliteration. What John sees is the creation purged by the searing light of Christ's judgement. So totally judged, so totally purged of what frustrates God's will, that even that most fundamental sign of the separation between God and God's creation – the distinction between heaven and earth – is now done away with. 'The tabernacle of God is among mortals', John hears a heavenly voice proclaim: God is fully at one with his people, so that heaven merges with earth. And this utter renewal of creation includes also our own transformation into people more glorious, more fully human, more open to God and transparent to the divine light, so as to cast out any lingering fear that the coming of Christ might mean that we will be any less ourselves.

Second, John sees the 'the new Jerusalem', *tēn Ierousalēm kainēn* in Greek. Note that John doesn't call it *Ierousalēm nea*, as if it were a new suburb of the old, like New Marston or New Hinksey, still less a brand-new replacement, such as New South Wales or Stevenage New Town. This is *Ierousalēm kainē*. It is renewed Jerusalem, transformed Jerusalem, but it is still Jerusalem. I find that very reassuring, given that all of us can probably identify specific places which have been particularly important in our lives, whether they be places of pilgrimage, or places that we call home, or places where our life was changed significantly. John's vision points to the possibility of these places being caught up and renewed in the new heaven and new earth.

Moreover, the new Jerusalem is not simply a place. It is also specifically a city. It is particularly significant that, in his ultimate vision, John sees the fulfilment of God's plan as a city, because cities are places of human culture, and human community, and human aspirations. True, this is the Jerusalem that God builds; but in building the new Jerusalem, God takes up and transfigures those human longings and that human desire to participate in his creativity.

Finally, John's vision gives us a hint that the new Jerusalem is not only something that we are waiting for with anticipation in the future. St Augustine in the *City of God* Book 20 seems to pick up on the present participle John uses: 'coming down'. The new Jerusalem does not simply come down at the end, but is already coming down out of heaven from God. Hence from earliest times, John's vision has also been interpreted as a vision of the Church. Which is one of the reasons why the architects of medieval cathedrals were so keen to model them on John's description of the new Jerusalem. And why visionaries like Blake – though in a very different way from the rather nostalgic use of his words by Middle England – have held that it might be possible to build Jerusalem even now, among the dark Satanic mills in England's green and pleasant land. If Advent is as much about those intermediate comings of Christ, then what might our lives look like, what might our churches look like and what might this House look like, if we took this Advent gift to heart: living as communities and as individuals on whom the new Jerusalem was already descending, renewing us and transforming us into the likeness of Christ?

The Christ who is Coming

St Mary Magdalene, Lincoln
Zephaniah 3.14–20; Philippians 4.4–7; Luke 3.7–18

ARABELLA MILBANK

The Gospel today takes us by surprise. In a strange inversion, all the gut-wrenching, pulpit-bashing terror is coming not from our reading in the prophetic books of the Old Testament – but from the New. It is in the Gospel that the people of God are admonished as a 'brood of vipers'. It is there that they, that we, are violently exhorted to repent, to return, to renew. It is there that we hear the bitter language of judgement by flood and by flame. And in Zephaniah, by contrast, there is sweetness and light. We have ringing choruses of song: 'Sing, aloud O Daughter Zion!' And again in the epistle, words echoing with the jubilance of Purcell's famous setting: 'Rejoice in the Lord alway … and again I say rejoice!'

To this festivity, John the Baptist comes as a party-pooper, pushing aside the tinsel, wielding a sharp-edged tongue with which to puncture our festive balloons, an axe to lay to the root of our early-erected Christmas trees. And what is more, he says there is what we can only presume is worse to come – that his words, his actions, his sacramental power are as insipid and cool as the water in which he baptizes when compared to the fire and Spirit of the 'one who is more powerful than I'.

And as later passages of Luke will reveal, he was right: John the Baptist tells us only to give away one coat if we have two, but

Christ tells the lawyer to give up all he has and follow him. John instructs the tax-collector and soldiers to pursue their professions with integrity; Christ tells the fishermen to transform their callings into the new vocation of discipleship.

When we speak of John the Baptist as the 'last of the Old Testament prophets', and associate him with the Advent Sunday between that proper to those prophets (Advent 2) and that dedicated to the Mother of God (Advent 4), we might seem to suggest a simple trajectory from violence to peace, from male to female, from the law to the spirit, from justice to mercy. Without today's Gospel, we might assume we turn our backs on doom-laden and forceful language, on talk of the polluted and oppressive city.

We most easily say that the messianic expectation voiced there and through the Baptizer is in some way 'wrong' – too warlike, too violent-heroic, this one 'whose winnowing fork is in his hand, to clear his threshing floor' (Matt. 3.12). (Even as in Zephaniah 'The Lord, your God, is in your midst, a warrior who gives victory.') No, it is surely a little baby we are waiting for, an image we know perhaps all too well, the tiny-tears baby doll in the cardboard manger, the 'holy infant, tender and mild' whose image we make in sugared dough when we wrap the stollen loaf around its marzipan.

But no again – he is both these things. Powerful beyond the feeble images of human language, tender beyond even the beautiful pictures every nativity scene paints. Mighty as the child's endlessly deserving need, her potential to love, make her mighty to rule over our hearts. Merciful as the cutting hand of a surgeon, opening the wound to heal. For the child of Bethlehem is also the one to come again, to see the desolate city of our hearts, to see the desolate cities that evil men and women have defaced or indeed destroyed: to see Raqqa, see Paris; see London and Rangoon, see Baghdad and San Bernardino, see Lincoln and Juba.

In our reading from Zephaniah we are given just the last chorus of joy, spared the images of devastation and the call to repentance with which that book is otherwise filled. But perhaps we feel hardly ready, in the face of the violence erupting on the face of our earth, as we hear the jets from RAF Coningsby preparing for war, to be the rejoicing city. Perhaps we are better served by John the Baptist.

How can we live Advent, trapped in our own inadequacy as we are, an inadequacy brought painfully close by our response to the sufferings, ills and needs of others, hardly ready to give away one coat, let alone all we have – asking with the crowds before John, 'what do we do with what you have told us?' Asking also, somewhere within us, of the preacher we hear and the gospel that burns through our hearts: 'are you really speaking of the "one who is to come", of the Messiah I know by love, I expect by love? Where, who, how is he to be?'

But we need not despair, for as the child is the judge, so the judge is the child. There was a tradition in the Middle Ages that at Christ's Second Advent he would come to judgement not simply in regal majesty, not even only displaying his wounds made by nails and spear, but actually on the cross. On the cross, Christ's body is as naked as we see him at the Nativity, stripped to the same yardage of white cloth that wrapped his infant form. On the wooden slats of the cross he is vulnerable, vulnerable as he is lying in the frame of the crib, the focus of a love that is moved tenderly, adoringly. On the cross he is the guiltless victim, guiltless as the child whose very birth makes him the hunted object of Herod's soldiers. On the cross, as in the manger, it is by Christ's very innocence that we are judged; confronted in that endlessly adorable and adoring face with all that we can be before God and our neighbour and perhaps are not yet.

Advent is a time of great promise, the promise of the coming of a great power of love, of a restoration of all things. At Christmas especially, as of course at every Eucharist, we are brought to gaze upon Christ's face in time as the possibility of the ultimate good emerging from within the ruins of history. When Zephaniah describes the desolate city, just before the breaking into song we heard in our reading today, he speaks of 'bare ruined choirs' of a sort, of 'cedar work … laid bare', of buildings reduced to rafters in which owls and ravens roost. He speaks of 'a place for herds to lie down', of an occupation by shepherds, of kings on their knees.

Does this perhaps remind you of something? Think of the

outline of the traditional crib scene, the stripped stable frame of wood. The beams open to the stars – and the angels. Think of the cow, the sheep, the donkey making their beds there, the herds lying down. It is here, in the stable that is also the image of the stripped and devastated city, we hear as in Zephaniah, a song sung by the daughter of Zion. Out of the desolation and the wilderness comes Mary's Magnificat, that song of gentle might, of merciful justice: 'My Spirit rejoices in God my Saviour ... He has filled the hungry with good things and sent the rich away empty' (Luke 1.47, 53). And to her God in his angels, and in his way, the child in the cradle, reply, as our prophet tells us: he 'joys over her with singing'.

Let us travel towards them, this Advent and always.

Waiting and Birthing

Fourth Sunday of Advent and Christmas Eve
St Margaret, Winnipeg, Manitoba
2 Samuel 7.1–5, 8–11, 16; Acts 13.16–26; Luke 1.67–79

KIRSTEN PINTO GFROERER

Blessed are you among women, and blessed is the fruit of your womb. (Luke 1.42)

Today is the morning of Mary and thus it is the morning of the Church: for she is our mother.

Mary is the beginning of the Church; she is the dwelling place of God with humanity. The Spirit prepared her in grace, and made room for the incarnation of the Triune God in her belly. In her 'the whole fullness of Godhead dwells bodily'. (Col. 2.9)

Listen to some words of John Donne to this our mother.

> *Salvation to all that will is nigh;*
> That all, which always is all everywhere …
> Which cannot die, yet cannot choose but die,
> Lo, faithful Virgin, yields himself to lie …
> *Immensity cloistered in thy dear womb.*[5]

The transcendent God, that 'all which always is all everywhere', allows himself to be 'cloistered in', identified with, our humanity. He does so likewise in the Church. Today and throughout history Mary and the Church have been entwined. You, the Church, are Mary and Mary is you. She is particular – only she is the God-bearer – but you are within her because you are within Him whom she bears.

Julian of Norwich in her *Revelations* describes these truths with elliptical brilliance:

> God knitted Himself to our body in the Virgin's womb … Thus our Lady is our Mother in whom we are all enclosed and of her born, in Christ: (for she that is Mother of our Saviour is Mother of all that shall be saved in our Saviour;) and our Saviour is our Very Mother in whom we be endlessly borne, and never shall come out of Him.[6]

Earlier she tries to describe these circles of indwelling in the Trinitarian life:

> We are enclosed in the Father, and we are enclosed in the Son, and we are enclosed in the Holy Ghost. And the Father is enclosed in us, and the Son is enclosed in us, and the Holy Ghost is enclosed in us: Almightiness, All-Wisdom, All-Goodness: one God, one Lord.[7]

'Immensity cloistered in thy dear womb.'

Remember, Church, on this morning on the cusp of Christmas: In you dwells the incarnate one, born and revealed and yet hidden from sight and coming again. You are his body, the Spirit is your breath. You are enclosed in him, he is enclosed in you, you are enclosed in her, in him. Wonderful isn't it?

'Immensity cloistered in thy dear womb.'

This Mary whom we contemplate this morning is with child, but her time has not yet come. She is waiting, and in haste she has gone to seek out her cousin Elizabeth. This waiting is decisive since nothing will come to pass without it. This Mary has given her assent to an angel to participate in the glorious mystery of love – 'behold the handmaid of the Lord: be it according to your will.' Mary's assent is not an agreement to act but rather an assent to hope that the promise to her might be fulfilled. It is an assent to wait for the Holy Spirit to overshadow her, for the power of God to come upon her that she might conceive and bear a Son. Just so, the Church has been asked to be that dwelling place for God, and to wait. And so the task of the preacher this morning is one of midwifery.

Advent for the Church is our time of waiting, our confinement, culminating in the travail of labouring with the mystery of Christ's incarnation and his coming again in Glory. As midwife, my work today is to ask you to attend to this labour. Please do not rush: it is early in the morning, hold back for a moment, do not push through too quickly to the miracle of Christmas. I beg you, don't push before your time, stay here waiting and let the Holy One do what he is doing and come as he will come. The waiting is imperative; it is the task of the Church. We must wait for the coming, live in the fervour of watching as one aching for the morning of her release, trembling with fear and awaiting the dawn.

A woman in labour bets her whole life on the promise of the coming. She is at risk, living in expectation of fulfilment. When the time comes, she can do nothing but breathe, wait, and persevere as the fruit of her womb does its work in her body. As the Church, our perseverance in this state never can count on its success, hoping that it may get easier or better. Perseverance aims only at the end, the hope of the return of the Incarnate One, Jesus Christ.

Is this waiting inactive? No. A woman growing with child and labouring to give birth exerts an enormous amount of energy. However, it is a passive form of action. The alien, other force inside of her shapes her body and prepares a dwelling place, and forces its way into the air.

In the Church it is the work of the Holy Spirit to prepare this Body with grace for her indwelling. He who fills this body is our Maker, our beginning and our end.

'*Immensity cloistered in thy dear womb*', oh Church. The Church is, because God is. The Church is Holy because God is Holy. And the holiness of the Church is at the heart of her holy active passivity, her waiting, and her reliance on the work of the Triune God.

Therefore we must understand today, on the fourth Sunday of Advent, on the cusp of Christmas, what it is to wait. In a world that attempts to obliterate the distance between God and humankind by sentimentalizing the story of Christ's incarnation and by de-emphasizing his coming again in judgement and finality, in a world that replaces penitence and waiting with celebration and consumption, in this world the Church needs to wait. Her gift to the world is this waiting. What the world needs is to witness her in the glow of pregnancy and the throes of labour, in burning expectation of her redemption.

'Blessed is she who believes that there would be a fulfil-ment of what was spoken to her by the Lord.'

John Webster says that it is God who speaks his name to us. And when this word is spoken we believe.

In anticipation of his coming we the labouring Church must wait in faith and this faith is an 'eschatological mode of existence, it is the surrender of all security in complete openness to the future'. [8] It is a self-securing sufficiency that shuts us off from the voice and action of the Godhead upon us. This craving for self-sufficiency is a turn from relationality, and assuredly one must move relationally to give birth. The way of self-sufficiency is anti-generative and anti-creative.

But only a proclamatory word spoken to us can free us from ourselves; a word that challenges us to live from God's future, the fruition of his work, his coming again in glory, a word that impregnates us and changes the shape of our being. In this way, as in the annunciation, pregnancy and birth of Mary, in this way indeed God happens to us.

To close let us consider one more image of our Mother, which may enrich the waiting; the image of Mary as the Ark of the Covenant. The Ark served also as a holy womb of the glory of God. In the Old Testament, the Ark of the Covenant was kept in the Holy of Holies. Only the high priest could enter this sacred place and only once a year. Once a year in fear and great joy he would come and worship and here he would say the name left unuttered for the rest of the year; the name of the Saviour God.

The Ark, unlike the manger scene, is difficult to sentimentalize or commercialize. People died when they touched the Ark irreverently. The priest who went into the Holy of Holies had a rope tied to his leg to ensure that he could be dragged out if he was slain by the glory. One imagines light streaming from the Ark, blinding and dangerous light, the glory of God. In legends of the birth of Christ, which coincide with this image, he emerges in a burst of light blinding all of those around. Though these stories may de-emphasize the real miracle of infinity coming into the humble human body, they point to a truth about this moment that must be held in tension with the fleshyness of it all. The God in Mary's womb is as immense, as transcendent and as awe-full as the God who dwelt among the people of the Ark. This baby born tonight is our Judge and King. Mary bore the one who would tear the veil of the Holy of Holies, who would offer a sacrifice once and for all, who harrows hell and who sits enthroned among the cherubim and seraphim as the propitiation for our sins. Mary bore the Glory of God.

And so now as the labour begins this morning, let us wait and prepare to enter the Holy of Holies with and in our High Priest and his Mother. Let us wait, in awe and pregnant expectation, betting our life on the promise of his coming. For tonight we will stand in him over the mercy seat of the Ark and he will breathe through us the confession of our sins, he will offer our liturgy as a sacrifice of praise and he will sprinkle his blood on us in the eucharistic feast. Let us wait and pray until the dawning when he will utter his own name through our lips and be birthed in our hearts once more. Amen.

II

Preaching Paradox:
Christmas to Candlemas

The Feast of the Nativity still fills churches up and down the land. But it is on the poetry, including that of carols, that we can found our theological exposition of the doctrine of the incarnation. It is time to end the downplaying of Christmas as sentimental and to release its evangelistic potential, which will come from a fuller presentation of its paradoxical truth: that the same child lying in an animal trough is the sustainer of the universe. It is no accident that the Methodist movement, with its empowering of lay vocation through the doctrine of sanctification, should have produced such a strongly incarnational hymn as Charles Wesley's 'Hark, the herald angels sing', whose line 'Veiled in flesh, the Godhead see, / Hail the incarnate Deity' speaks of a humanity that mystically reveals the divinity. For the paradox of the union of the two natures in Christ speaks to our own paradoxical condition. As Pascal avowed, we are both beast and angel, and the mystical exchange of Christ's two natures is what makes our salvation possible.

The whole period between Christmas and Candlemas is one great cycle of discovery of this doctrine and the anthropology that proceeds from it, including especially through the Feast of the Baptism of Christ. Epiphany also explores the cosmic implications of the incarnation; as such it is the opportunity for joyful proclamation of creation as revealing by its complex interconnections the splendour of the overflowing Divine life. The imagery of light, which is so central to the season, encourages us to see the created order as a scintillating sequence of mirrors, reflecting the divine radiance. The Presentation feast, which ends this section, is set within the Temple, which was for its people the image of the splendour of the whole created order, with its Creator at its heart.

'Word without a word'

Feast of the Nativity
Southwell Minster
Hebrews 1.1–12; John 1.1–14 (AV)

THE REVD DR ALISON MILBANK

Words, words, words. Our lives are swathed in too many words. The internet has vastly extended the numbers of words produced: in blogs, news and chat-rooms. One of the joys for me at Christmas is putting a 'gone away' reply on my email, to stem the outpouring of message after message. But the word is the way St John's Gospel introduces the incarnation, God with us, and our epistle reading too is about words: those spoken by God 'in sundry times and in diverse manners'. The writer of Hebrews is going through a selection of God's words in Scripture, which, he argues, look forward to Christ, and make him greater than the angels. He is working his way towards the great truth that the Church holds out to the world, that the child Jesus is God's own Son, but he marshals text after text in a verbal battery that is quite dizzying.

It all slows down for us in that great poem of the Gospel opening: 'In the beginning was the Word, and the Word was with God, and the Word was God.' You cannot say it quickly but have to pause, let the weight of it sink in, allow the silence to speak. For God's speech is different from ours. Our words come quickly or slowly from our lips and pass away. Yesterday's newsprint goes in the recycling bin; a tweet twitters and is gone. Our speech hysterically fills a vacuum. But God's speech is what holds us in being; you and I and the universe are swathed in God's breath.

Creation did not happen and stop like our words but is a constant activity. And the Word, the Son shapes that breath into forms of life, like you and me.

At the Nativity, that Word became an infant, kept warm by the breath of animals. The famous seventeenth-century preacher Lancelot Andrewes spoke of the *Verbum infans* – the infant or unspeaking word: 'the Word without a word, the eternal Word not able to speak a word, a wonder sure and swaddled; and that a wonder too. He that takes the sea "and rolls it about the swaddled bands of darkness" to come thus into clouts/cloths himself'.[9] Andrewes loves the paradoxes of the baby in the swaddling clothes being the one who swaddled the darkness of chaos, the baby who is the Word, an infant, who can only cry. And we too are spellbound by this mystery.

But there is a further paradox here. Yes, baby Jesus is an infant, but in him God has already spoken: he is God's speech. All that God has to communicate lies here. He makes himself weak, vulnerable, yet with all the awe-inspiring fresh perfection of a baby.

That is God's Word, who allows himself to be wrapped in swaddling bands, and will clothe himself in our grief, our sorrow, our anger – the only answer Christianity offers to the mystery of suffering. We hold up a child: God's speech. In that baby, he communicates more deeply than our millions of words, and that is why we make our best response in poetry, song and silence, which are all modes that point to the limits of our speech.

So, I also end in this way, with Thomas Pestel's seventeenth-century poem:

> Behold the great Creator makes
> himself a house of clay,
> a robe of virgin flesh he takes
> which he will wear for ay.
>
> Hark, hark, the wise eternal Word,
> like a weak infant cries!

In form of servant is the Lord,
and God in cradle lies.[10]

Surprised by Joy

Feast of the Epiphany
Southwell Minster
Isaiah 60.1–6; Ephesians 3.1–12; Matthew 2.1–12

THE REVD DR ALISON MILBANK

One of the many joys of having a grandchild is revisiting customs and games devised for your children. My grandson loves to move the wooden wise men a bit nearer each day to our home nativity, just as his mother once did. It is a bit of a squash fitting everyone in the stable, but without the wise men the scene – and our Christmas joy – would not be complete. Their story, however, is of a different order to that of the shepherds. Shepherds are local and natural visitors; even today, with new settlements towering over Bethlehem, shepherds still pasture animals on the Judaean hills. We know that the ordinary Jewish people were longing for a Saviour, but where do wise men fit in? What are they doing in this most Jewish-focused Gospel of Matthew? What especial joy do they bring?

Although they may appear like figures from a fairy-story like Aladdin, their background is solidly historical. Magi were priest scholars of the Zoroastrian religion, originating from what is now Iran. They used astrology to measure time but did not believe the stars fixed your destiny. They may easily have known the prophecy of Balaam in Numbers 24 about a star coming out of Jacob and a sceptre out of Israel, and nations then had constellations that represented them: Israel was Aries. Matthew may have included their story as a fulfilment of the prophecy of Isaiah 60.3 in which kings journey towards the radiance of the holy city. For he consistently presents Christ as the coming true of all the Jewish hopes and prophecies. The words of the prophets were directed to expectations of their own time – here a restored Jerusalem – but Christians believe that they spoke more than they knew: for us the whole Old Testament witnesses to Jesus. His coming suddenly makes its pieces fit together like a jigsaw. Matthew did not make the magi up – if he had invented the story he would have made the visitors kings not astrologers. We only call them kings because later people tried to fit them to the Isaiah reading. For Matthew, they are the witness of the world beyond Judaism to the Messiah, building on the tradition that even a Persian king like Cyrus could be an instrument of God's providence. Sometimes legend has made them of different races to show that Jesus is for all humankind. So our first joy is that in the foreign Magi, we non-Jews have our part in the nativity: Jesus gives himself to the whole world.

The second joy comes from the beliefs of the Magi. It was no accident that it was Zoroastrians who arrived because of all the faiths at the time, they alone shared the Jewish belief that God is one. They follow the star because they too believe in a coming Saviour. But also because they see the stars as exemplary of the wise order of the cosmos God has made: their Creator is called Ahura Mazda – 'Wise Lord'. We see in Zoroastrianism the way all faiths search after the truth and how the Christ Child offers a fulfilment of what is good in them. The wisdom of the Magi is symbolic of the value of a philosophical reaching out to truth through our natural reason and observation. From the beginning, human ways of seeing Christ are multiple: for the Jewish shepherds, illumination comes from angels; for the wise men, the light of reason.

But the Magi's is also a dualist belief: Ahura Mazda is shadowed by a dark rival, a force of destruction, much more powerful than the Christian idea of the evil one. They therefore walk in darkness like the nations in Isaiah 60.2. And yet they discover through following the star, prophesied in the Jewish Scriptures, a way of overcoming this darkness, and to believe in the triumph of goodness, just as the arrival of the wise men reveals to the Jewish context that the expected Saviour is for more than themselves. Christ welcomes all truth in human religious searching, and that is our second joy – all roads to truth will one day lead to the stable. You may be only uncertainly on the journey but your seeking is itself a holy thing, if you open yourself to new ideas and being changed by them.

We today are again in thrall to a belief in the power of evil and negativity. We live in a time of great uncertainty, insecurity and fear of what the future might bring. Sometimes we too cling like the ancient Jews to an exclusiveness as a defence against a terrifying world. We will not have true joy unless we ourselves follow the star.

The wise men set off on a journey to an unknown destination but trusting in the cosmic order of the stars, the gift of the wise Creator, and they found the joy of all that they had been seeking. They worshipped – they prostrated themselves on the ground – which is why Christians have knelt ever since. They saw and believed the unsearchable mystery of Christ hidden in God until this moment. Everything they had longed for had come true, like the best fairy-stories, while their world was turned upside down because it was true and real: a baby with soft skin and a piercing cry. They had an epiphany. Everyone who reached the stable had one: even the angels were surprised. We tend to think angels know everything, but God's plan for humankind was, Ephesians says, a surprise for the 'rulers and principalities' – that is God's spiritual creation – as it was for the wise men who sought their saviour at a palace.

If we are to have an epiphany, the joy that tightens our chest and makes us want to cry or shout, we need to be ready to have our dreams come true: for all the goodness, beauty and truth of God to be real for us in love so true and fierce it will never let us down or let us go. And we must be ready like the wise men and the angels – and the prophets – to be surprised: to find strength where we least thought to find it, kindness in an enemy, blessing in the darkest of places, to believe that though darkness seems to cover the earth, the glow of God's love at its core is strong and steady in the candid eyes of the Christ Child.

Music and What Matters Most

Merton College Chapel, Oxford
1 Samuel 16; Psalm 150; Ephesians 1

THE REVD DR ANDREW DAVISON

My first secondary school music lesson was unusual, and it is unusual that I remember it in such vivid detail. The teacher began by singling me out with a difficult question: 'Andrew, is music the most important subject in the timetable?' I sat in silence for a moment, considered my options, and answered 'No'. My heart thumped. Had I offended the teacher? Thankfully not: he agreed with me, music is *not* the most important subject I would study. I came away with form points for honesty and courage.

But if I were asked again, I would be bolder. I would sidestep the question and say that music is an irreplaceable image of that which matters most. There, I am in good company among theologians. Martin Luther said that nothing is so much like grace as the music of Josquin des Prez. Karl Barth found in the music of Mozart much of what his own theology spelt out.

Music somehow touches on things of the highest importance, which is why we find it at the most significant times of life. People want music at weddings and at funerals. They want it to celebrate, and they want it to comfort them in the face of sadness and disintegration. We see that in our readings. It is no accident that David soothes the anguish of Saul with music from his lyre, or that Psalm 150, written for some great occasion of celebration, should call upon the whole ancient Hebrew orchestra.

Music can be an image of hope, compassion or redemption. Now, the question of *meaning* in music is famously tricky. How does music concern itself with what concerns us? I will pass over the use of imitation, with music evoking birdsong or the sounds of war, although that is part of the picture. I will also take it for granted, although it is difficult to explain how, that music can evoke certain emotions: through the sadness of the minor mode, the cheerfulness of the major, the poignancy of certain intervals, or the associations of certain keys.

I will pass them over because they are too static, and the seriously theological side of music comes in its relation to time, development and change. It is in *this* way that music concerns itself with those temporal matters that are so interwoven with value in human life: with sameness, repetition and difference; change and stability; interweaving and support; tension and resolution. These make up the texture of music, just as they make up the texture of a human life.

It is through these mainly structural elements that music presses upon matters closest to the human heart: upon fullness and emptiness, sadness and joy, determinacy and indeterminacy. It deals with them in ways familiar to us: in terms of change and evolution, of departure and return, of sameness and difference, of expectation, fulfilment and the unexpected. These are all theological matters.

Let me offer an example from the first movements of many of Haydn's symphonies. The themes presented at the beginning are developed, and then return in the recapitulation, towards the close. Just when we think that this has run its course, Haydn typically ratchets the music up to a new level, and we encounter so much more than we could have expected. Departure, and return with unexpected abundance: music is saying something fundamental here, which theology also wants to say.

In the parish where I served my curacy, I started a congregational hymn-singing practice, trying to teach some theology and something about music on the back of it. My best success came with *Now the Green Blade Riseth*, which we sing to the tune *Noël Nouvelet*. We worked out that the pattern of the tune is AABA.

But is that last line *really* the same as the beginning, after the episode of difference that has come in between? Yes, it is the same, they said, but in a way it isn't: it has a new meaning because of what had happened in between. We had encountered difference, repetition and transfiguration, all great theological subjects. Even the *same* is never the *same*: it is not the *same* because it is *again*. Music leads us to encounter old things in a new light.

That, indeed, is close to the essence of composition: to taking a musical idea and showing us its potential. Rather than discarding a seemingly insignificant motif, a composer might pay particular attention to it, and show us what can be found there. I hold Brahms dear for exactly this reason. Some idea, that you think he has cast aside, will come back and show itself to be of the first importance. I think of his violin concerto. There is the ethics of attention here, but also the deeply theological idea of an inexhaustible life and meaning to everything.

Music may even be said to provide parables of forgiveness. What is forgiven is not in any obvious sense undone. The past cannot be changed. The task in redemption is to transfigure the meaning of that which has happened. One cannot glibly say 'forgive and forget' to someone who still bears scars. The slow work of redemption and forgiveness is harder and more glorious than mere forgetting: it is about understanding that past in a different light, so as to remake its meaning. Music provides us with an image of this – only an image, but an image nonetheless.

As I end this sermon, I want to bring it round to Christ. How can Christians speak of compassion, or of forgiveness or redemption without speaking of Christ?

Music unfolds the possibilities that lie within its chosen musical themes. Christ, the true man, the one who is fully human, shows us of what human life is capable. If human history were like a sonata, then it would seem that Christ is the development – the section where the musical material is allowed to show its potential and stretch its wings. But, in fact, that English name for the middle of sonata form, 'development', is deceptive. It is not always about growth. Often it is about fragmentation and breaking apart. Harmonically, it involves wandering away from what has been set out at the start.

Perhaps, then, the coming of Christ is more like the final part of a piece in sonata form, the recapitulation, where the fragments are put back together. But even reassembled, they can never be the same. That evening around the piano in my old parish proved that: even the same is not the same when it is *again*, when something has happened in between. More often than not, a composer makes this clear: the end has a transcendent quality. Something in the instrumentation or the harmony bathes the musical material in a new light – and that cannot be separated from the journey we have been on, from having seen our musical subjects from many angles. The healing of all things by Christ is surely like that.

One of the greatest Church Fathers, St Irenaeus of Lyons, knew all about this. He used the very word to describe the coming of Christ that we use (at least as it comes into English) for the end of a movement such as this: recapitulation. God, Irenaeus said, had entered into every stage of human life, sanctifying it and vivifying it with divinity. Christ had drawn all things to himself. Irenaeus was meditating upon the words we heard from Ephesians, words which described God's plan for redemption in Christ: 'to gather up all things in Christ, things in heaven and things on earth'.

To recapitulate, to gather up in Christ: this is Irenaeus' vision of unity, peace and community, of humanity drawn together and united to God in Christ. Thereafter, the Church, his body, is to be this site of unity, peace and community. God has joined himself to us in our flesh, to retrieve our loss by summing up all things in the incarnate Son.

Music can be an expression of this hope – that from this world of time and change, of fragmentation and loss there may be a gathering together and a reinterpretation. Music is not in itself salvific, but it bears a most eloquent witness to the One who is: and to him, to Christ our Lord, may praise of music be made, now and in eternity.

The Cold Water of Baptism

Baptism of Our Lord
St Barnabas Cathedral, Nottingham
Isaiah 55.1–11; 1 John 5.1–9; Mark 1.7–11

FR JOSEPH VNUK

I know a Dominican sister from the Solomon Islands – Sister Rita is her name. She grew up in a fishing village, and the people would often swim in the sea, which was pleasantly warm all year round. Even after her religious profession, she and her fellow-sisters would go down to the beach from time to time and enjoy the balmy waters. Now, at one stage she had to go to Australia for some meetings, and the Dominican sisters there took her to visit some of their communities, even as far south as Tasmania. One winter's day they were driving along the Tasmanian coast, and as she saw the sea shining in the winter sun, it reminded her of the sea she knew back in the Solomons. So she got out and got herself ready for a quick dip. She ran down to the waves that looked so welcoming and plunged herself in. I shall not attempt to describe the total shock she experienced when she met instead the chill waters of the Antarctic Ocean. A life spent entirely in the tropics, where you could only meet cold water in glasses and bottle – assuming you were lucky enough to have electricity and a fridge – had left her totally unprepared for being surrounded by an ocean of it. You and I have lived in cold countries. We expect the water to be cold, and we brace ourselves for it, or gingerly dip our toes in to test, or perhaps wait until a braver friend has taken the plunge first, who can then say to us, 'The water's fine. Come on in!'

If we want an image to help us understand the Feast of the Baptism of Christ, the feast we celebrate today, then that is a good place to start: if we have suspicions and hesitations about the waters of baptism, then Jesus helps us by being baptized himself, and saying 'The water's fine. Come on in!' It is an image to start with; we need to explore it a little. For a start, almost all of us have been baptized already, most of us while we were still too young to be aware of what was happening, so plunging into the waters of baptism is not an issue for us. Even if it were, it is not the coldness of the water that would frighten us, but other things.

But even if we were baptized as infants, this does not mean that baptism is something over and done with in the past. Each day we are asked to live as baptized people, to re-affirm our identity as beloved children who live in the good pleasure of God. Every time we come into the church we renew our commitment to baptism by blessing ourselves with holy water in the name of the Trinity. And this affirmation of our baptism is not something automatic: we all know people who used to come to church but no longer do so; some of you here find it difficult to make a weekly commitment, or perhaps you come, but in some other area of your life your behaviour is not really that of a beloved child of God.

Many of us were like Sister Rita: in our childhood the waters of baptism were warm and welcoming; it felt comforting to be part of the Church. Perhaps suddenly, as for Sister Rita, perhaps gradually, as in many cases, the waters have grown cold and uninviting. And if it has not been part of your spiritual journey so far, then it may happen at some time in the future. How can the baptism of Jesus help us?

First, it helps us to focus our attention on Jesus. In our readings today the prophecies of Isaiah point us to Jesus; the letters of St John the Evangelist point us to Jesus; John the Baptist points us to Jesus; the voice of the Father points us to Jesus, and the Holy Spirit as a dove points out Jesus. People may have difficulties with the Pope, Church, with Christianity, with the Bible, and with God, but almost all of them still have some attraction, some devotion, to Jesus. So, in any crisis of faith, it is important to keep our eyes fixed on Jesus.

Above all, what attracts people to Jesus is that Jesus welcomes them. Jesus heals them and comforts them and forgives them and drives away the spirits that torment them. Jesus does this not just for the respectable and the holy, but for the outcasts and the marginalized: the lepers, the unclean, the tax collectors, the disgraced women, the sinners. And finally, Jesus is prepared to die for them. If Jesus is harsh on anyone, it is on those who would interfere with this welcome and fellowship: the synagogue officials who want to prevent him from healing on the Sabbath; the scribes and teachers who complain when he pronounces forgiveness; the Pharisees who grumble when he eats with sinners; and even his own disciples when they drive away the little children. Who could not feel welcomed by someone who is so welcoming? Who could possibly want to turn away from him?

What we celebrate on this feast is the extraordinary depth of this welcome. Many of you will have found yourself talking to some politician or civic official, and as you expressed your concerns to them you would have found them very welcoming, very sympathetic to what you had to say. But it's all PR; there is no real commitment; they walk away and leave you to yourself. John the Baptist spoke out against all that was wrong in his society, and urged people to change, to repent of their sins. To be baptized by John was to accept his critique and to express solidarity with all those who were similarly moved by it. It was a very real and public gesture of commitment and belonging to a group of people over whom Jesus had no control. It is a humbling step. But it is precisely when Jesus makes this humbling step, when his welcome of other people goes beyond a smile to real commitment, it is then that the Father acknowledges him as his true Son.

Even John the Baptist was taken aback at this humility. The evangelists tried to minimize it. The preachers and writers of the early Church were embarrassed by it. Why should the sinless One submit to a baptism of repentance? The answer they gave was that Jesus was not made holy by the water of his baptism, but rather in submitting to baptism Jesus made the water of baptism holy.

We probably take it for granted that when babies are baptized something holy happens to them. But we do at times find it difficult to believe that keeping our identity as baptized people is going to keep us holy. We can look at the Church around us and ask if we might not be holier by getting out of the Church rather than being contaminated by the people who are in it: priests who commit child abuse, Catholics who kill Protestants in Ireland; the decadent popes of the Renaissance; and those individual Catholics whom we have known –priests, sisters, religion teachers, perhaps even our parents – whose lives were marked by fear, hypocrisy, lack of forgiveness, or maybe just wacky ideas. Surely we lose our holiness by expressing our solidarity with people like these? The waters of baptism look very cold and uninviting.

But the two Johns remind us that Jesus has come with both water and the Holy Spirit. The water that connects us with other people is made warm by the fire of the Holy Spirit. Our connection to all these dubious people is a connection in Christ. We become holy by connecting with them, not because we are approving all their misdeeds, but because we are imitating Jesus. It is when we have taken our plunge into this sea of humanity in Christ that we are acknowledged as a true child of God, someone whose holiness lies in humility and solidarity.

Sister Rita still enjoys swimming. We too can keep splashing ourselves with holy water and living the life of the baptized, if we keep in mind that above all our commitment is not to the sins of the sinners, but to Jesus who welcomes all, even sinners.

In particular we ratify our baptismal commitment by sharing in the Eucharist. It is precisely in our union with Jesus here that we also become one body with the others whom Jesus welcomes. And the more open we are when we receive the Eucharist, the more easily we shall hear God say to us 'This is my son, the beloved'. And then we shall truly give praise to the Father, through the Son, in the Holy Spirit, to whom be all honour and glory for ever and ever.

Amiably Drawn

Second Sunday of Epiphany
St Andrew's Church, Handsworth, Birmingham
1 Samuel 3; John 1.43–51

THE REVD CANON DR EDMUND NEWEY

What was it that made you come to church this morning? What got you out of bed on a cold and rainy day to come here to St Andrew's? If this were a school assembly, I'm fairly sure it wouldn't take long to get an answer. When the Vicar comes to school and asks questions, the children quickly learn that there are two expected answers: God and Jesus! Who made the world? God did. Whose birthday is it at the end of December? Jesus'. It doesn't always work, though. I well remember the second time I went into a school in my old parish. It was only a few weeks since I'd first been introduced to the children, so I thought I would begin by asking them if they could remember my name. 'Good morning, children. It's lovely to be here again. I wonder if any of you can remember my name...' *A long silence... No hands went up...* Finally at the back an arm was tentatively raised: 'Are you Jesus?'!

But what about my first question? What was it that made you come to church this morning? Probably all of us think that the right answer must be one of those two: God or Jesus. But, if that *is* the right answer, then I suspect we're all feeling a little bit guilty. After all, if we're honest, most of us have a variety of motivations for being here today.

We're here *out of habit*, because that's how we've always spent our Sunday mornings.

Or we're here to *see our friends*. One of the nicest things people say about a church is that it's such a friendly place that it feels like home. Many of us feel like that about St Andrew's – it's our home from home, a place where we feel safe in the company of friends.

Or perhaps you're new here – here for the first or second time. You've gone past the church on the bus, you've heard about it from friends, and, *out of curiosity*, you've decided to give it a try.

And, if those are some of the reasons you are here, the first thing to say is that there's absolutely nothing wrong with that. Very often the answer to a question isn't an either/or, but a both/and. If you've come to church out of habit, or to see our friends, or out of curiosity (or even, like me, because it's your job), that doesn't mean that you're not also here because of God and Jesus too. 'God works in mysterious ways/ His wonders to perform.' And one of the most mysterious of all is that God works through the normal everyday things of life: through our routines and our friends and our natural inclinations. When God calls us it is not always by portents in the heavens. Often, it's by small and everyday things – a smile or a chance, kind word. There's a lovely turn of phrase for this from the great Anglican theologian, Richard Hooker: we are not compelled by God, he says, we are 'amiably drawn' – attracted, that is, by the friendly face of God, who draws us gently nearer.

God's grace does not destroy our human nature, it perfects it. God works *with* the grain, not *against* it. 'What woman', Jesus says, 'having ten silver coins, if she loses one of them, does not light a lamp, sweep the house and search carefully until she finds it?' (Luke 15.8). One good way of reading that story is to see the house as our human nature and the coins as the gifts God gives us, which in the course of life it is so easy to lose or squander. The way to regain those gifts is not to tear the house down. It is to light a lamp, the light that Christ brings us, and, in its brightness, to sweep clean the messy household of our lives until what we have lost is returned to us. 'When she has found it, she calls together her friends and neighbours, saying, "Rejoice with me, for I have found the coin that I had lost". Just so, I tell you, there is joy in the presence of the angels of God over one sinner who repents' (Luke 15.9–10).

In our first reading we heard about the boy Samuel, 'ministering to the LORD under Eli'. 'The word of the Lord was rare in those days', the Bible tells us, 'visions were not widespread'. And why was Samuel there in the Temple? Not because he had chosen to be, not because he had heard God's call himself. He was there because his mother Hannah had dedicated him to the Lord. All her life she had been despised as a childless woman, and when, in her old age, she gave birth to a son, she promised him to the Lord from the day that he was weaned. So, from as long ago as he could remember, the Temple had been Samuel's dwelling place, where he lived and worked and played, the place he called his home. If you had asked him why he was there, it's most unlikely that this 12-year-old boy would have said it had anything to do with God. He was there because his mother said so. In fact, the book of Samuel tells us this: 'Now Samuel did not yet know the LORD, and the word of the LORD had not yet been revealed to him'. So, when God speaks, Samuel doesn't know how to hear. The Lord calls to Samuel, 'Samuel, Samuel'. Samuel hears and answers, 'Here I am', but it's Eli to whom he runs. Again the Lord calls, 'Samuel, Samuel'. 'Here I am', he replies and runs once more to Eli. It's only at the third time of asking that Eli realizes what might be happening: 'Go, lie down; and if he calls you, you shall say, "Speak, LORD, for your servant is listening"'.

Very often it's like that for us too. 'The word of the Lord is rare in our days', we think to ourselves; 'visions are not widespread'. Yet, if we spend time in the place where we have been sent, if we listen to the voices and the advice of those around us, if we let *habit* and *friends* and *curiosity* do their work, then God will speak to us just as he spoke to Samuel.

Today's second reading was from John's Gospel. Nathanael is a prickly sort of character. Dragged along by his friend Philip to meet Jesus, he's not exactly over-enthusiastic: 'can anything good come out of Nazareth?' Yet, if only out of curiosity, he goes along. But, whatever he thought his motivation was, as soon as he meets Jesus he realizes the answer to the question of why he is there. 'Rabbi,' he says, 'you are the Son of God! You are the King of Israel!' But even that isn't quite right and Jesus tells him why. It is not the fact that Jesus is the Son of God that is most important, but that Jesus is the Son of Man. Jesus, the Son of Man, is the one who shows us what our human nature really looks like when it isn't disfigured by sin – what we humans might look like were we perfectly to reflect the image of God. God's grace does not destroy our human nature, it perfects it. God in Christ comes not to abolish but to fulfil and when we meet him a new vision opens up before us of life in all its fullness:

'Very truly, I tell you,' says Jesus, 'you will see heaven opened and the angels of God ascending and descending on the Son of Man.'

The Road to Insight

Conversion of St Paul
Pembroke College, Cambridge
Isaiah 49; Acts 9

SILVIANNE ASPRAY

Tonight is the eve of the Feast day of the Conversion of the Apostle
Paul. Some of you might be familiar with Caravaggio's paintings
of the scene: St Paul, after having been flung from his horse, lies
on the ground, facing the sky – illuminated and blinded alike by
a bright light from above. Caravaggio painted the scene twice,
as did numerous other artists through the ages, and I can easily
imagine why: the persecutor of Christians is turned around to
be an apostle in a remarkable scene involving some heavenly
pyrotechnics. What painter's imagination would not be captured
by the dramatic tension of this moment?

Yet there is also a much quieter side to Paul's conversion. It
is one that is easily forgotten amidst the drama of heavenly
voices, whinnying horses and the not-so-gentle landing of our
apostle-to-be: St Paul does not quite emerge from the ditch as
a newly illuminated, fully fledged apostle to the Gentiles. No,
the experience on the road to Damascus leaves him, first of all,
blind – and without much of a clue as to what is going to happen
next. Isn't this remarkable? Here we have a divine epiphany, but
– contrary to anything one would expect – the man to whom the
divine revelation is addressed is not illuminated, but left in the
dark. Rather than gaining a special insight, he is blinded. This
remarkable turn of the story suggests, I think, that the conversion

of St Paul did not really happen with a fall from a horse and a voice from heaven. This was only its beginning. St Paul's real conversion happens when his servant takes him by the hand and guides him, the blind man, towards Damascus. Here, and in his encounter with Ananias in Damascus, St Paul learns to let go of control and to trust in God and others.

Here is a man who started off his journey to Damascus knowing exactly what he was going to do: arrest some members of this sect called the Christians and bring them back to Jerusalem for their just punishment. He is the kind of guy who knows what he wants, who has a plan and who generally is on top of the situation.

And all of a sudden he no longer has a clue about what will happen next. Yes, he knows that he still has to go to Damascus – so much Jesus had told him in the apparition. But it is entirely unclear what will happen after he gets there. Where should he go? What should he do? St Paul does not have a plan any more; he is no longer in control. He knows little or nothing about this new vocation of his. It is only through his encounter with Ananias in Damascus that he will learn that God has called him to be an apostle to the Gentiles.

As if this loss of control had not been enough for poor St Paul, he also loses his sight. It is hard to imagine just how destabilizing this must have been. Completely blind, he has to take the hand of his servant, hold fast onto it like a small child, and have the servant guide him to Damascus. He who was used to leading others is now dependent on someone else's guidance. It must have been awkward. More than that: pretty humbling.

To let go of control, and to trust in the guiding hand of others and of God: that is the quiet side of St Paul's conversion. It is less spectacular, but it is no less important than the Caravaggio-moment. It is this experience, I think, that ultimately shapes Saul into St Paul. And this experience, moreover, is something that every believer faces, day by day: to let go of control, to put all trust in God, and to learn to see God's guiding in the community and people around.

We can go even one step further, and see in the quiet side of St Paul's conversion not only a model for the Christian life, but more generally a model for how learning works altogether. I am not talking here about the kind of learning that is a mere accumulation of facts, but about a kind of learning that is the beginning of wisdom. This kind of learning is what every university ought to strive for – and I know of many teachers in this college and beyond who give their all to achieve this in their students. But how exactly does one acquire this kind of learning?

Try to think of a moment of exceptional clarity, a light-bulb moment – and ask yourself how this came about. Isn't it often that these moments come after times of blindness, confusion and endless going round in circles? Don't we often go forward by what at first looks like falling back? Just like St Paul, who first had to go through a period of blindness, before the full scope of the Damascus road experience became clear to him in the encounter with Ananias.

Times of confusion and blindness are, of course, not always followed by moments of insight and clarity. Yet they nonetheless always teach us something about what is likely to be the right attitude in the face of the mystery of the world. Moments of blindness teach us – as they did St Paul – that a sense of complete control is ultimately illusionary. On the road to greater insight and wisdom, a sense of our own limits and a genuine humbleness is a better counsel than an inflated illusion of mastery.

Moreover, on the way to true insight, we need guides, and sometimes these may not be the ones we would expect to guide us. It would have been easy for St Paul to take an angel's hand and follow him to Damascus. Following his own servant, however, was much trickier. Similarly, it might be relatively easy for us to follow the advice of a big name in our field of study, or to trust the word of a friend we value. Are we prepared, however, to be guided by an unlikely guide? Like the lady who cleans the library? Are we ready to see wisdom in what people tell us, especially people whom we do not tend to look up to?

Having established that St Paul's conversion is about more than divine pyrotechnics, let me nonetheless return once again to the Caravaggio-moment of our story. We are told, after all, about a dramatic breaking in of God's presence. Is this not also a way in which God works in Paul's life, quite apart from teaching him how to be humble?

I personally do not doubt that dramatic epiphanies like the one St Paul experienced can happen, neither do I wish to de-mythologize what Scripture witnesses here. Yet there is a danger in focusing too much on extraordinary events like this one, when thinking about how God relates to this world. The danger is that we forget that God does not really need to break into our reality from beyond to be present here, because he already is at the core of it all anyway. And it is here that the lesson from Isaiah balances the account of St Paul's conversion in a very important way. The poem about God's servant we heard earlier can be read as bearing on St Paul. 'The LORD called me before I was born', we heard, 'while I was in my mother's womb he named me' (Isa. 49.1). It was only from St Paul's human perspective that the event on the road to Damascus seemed like a radical change. From God's perspective, he had called St Paul already before he was born. Indeed, God had 'formed [him] in the womb to be his servant' (Isa. 49.5). God is the creator and sustainer of all being, and as such, God is always already at the heart of all being. And this presence is precisely why the world has a depth that ultimately eludes our mastery, and it is also why any earthly being can guide us towards the transcendent God who is at its very core.

Splendour with No Bounds

Week of Prayer for Christian Unity
Westminster Cathedral

THE RIGHT REVD DR MARTIN WARNER

Light from Light, true God from true God, begotten not made, of one Being with the Father.

His eyes opened wide as he spoke. 'Light,' he said, 'the art of mosaic is the art of light. It is in the setting of the pieces, not in the colour. We see where one colour ends and another begins, but light is splendour, and splendour has no bounds.'

Words from the Nicene creed, and words from a novel by Barry Unsworth, improbably entitled *The Ruby in Her Navel*.[11] They are spoken by the most accomplished mosaicist of the twelfth century, Demetrius Karamides. I thought that mosaics might be a good subject to reflect on as a citizen of London, since both St Paul's Cathedral and Westminster Cathedral, which many people know well, are both distinguished by, among other things, their mosaics.

From the first time I was brought to visit Westminster Cathedral, a wondrous and enigmatic building, I have been captivated by its expression of Christian art and architecture that encompasses the traditions of both East and West. In the dim light of its chapels, aisles and ambulatories one detects in the mosaics an iconic quality of decoration that articulates faith and opens our minds to heaven in presenting us with the features of the saints. But as these visual images cluster around the lower reaches of J. F. Bentley's masterpiece, what also captures my imagination is the black expanse of brickwork in the ceiling, an apparently empty space that seems infinite, a symbolic expression of the profound unknowing that is indeed on earth an inescapable element in our search for God and for holiness.

By contrast, the mosaics in St Paul's are located precisely in the ceiling spaces of Wren's austerely baroque building, a scientific meditation on a vast scale on the metaphysics of time and eternity. Here the mosaic images, added heroically in the nineteenth century, are statements of faith that narrate the mystery of the eternal and are remote, majestic and apocalyptic. Creation and redemption, death, judgement, and the means of salvation hover above us in the eastern bays of the Quire as each day in the opus Dei of worship we seek to blend our voices with the eternal canticle of praise in heaven. *Benedicite, alleluia* is the refrain that echoes from the ceiling, while we below struggle to engage with the temporalities of life in the world's biggest trading centre for a global economy that is characterized by astonishing injustice and apparently invincible indifference to the reality of the invisible God whose beauty and power are revealed in poverty, suffering and hideous mutilation.

So here we are, two buildings, the masterpieces of their creators, each of which narrates in mosaic form something profound about the nature of our Christian discipleship and experience: whether in the nearness of heaven communicating its unknowableness, or the eternal claims of divine mercy and justice to which we are not yet fully conformed.

Although the mosaics play an indispensable part in the communication of both messages, there is something yet more profound within them that speaks to us about the gift of unity that is the particular intention of this Week of Prayer.

'Light is splendour and splendour has no bounds', says Demetrius Karamides. Everything about our human life has limitation; it is in some way incomplete, or as St Paul famously puts it, 'now we see through a glass darkly' (1 Cor. 13.12). And it is in this context that I take comfort from the fact that the two great churches in which we worship the eternal God are both, in some way, incomplete.

William Blake Richmond went to his grave mourning the fact that he was never able to complete the mosaics in St Paul's. And here, the work of completing the decorative scheme of mosaics and frescoes is being courageously continued. In both places we discover a parable about ourselves. It tells us that completion, that which finally bestows unity, revealing perfect truth and beauty in the vision of God, is God's gift, the goal and hope of all our striving, and the model to which our life must be conformed.

At present, we live all too often with our attention on where the colours begin and end, on the boundaries of colour that may provide invaluable definition, contrast and subtlety, but that are conditioned by the fragmentation of our life by time. Called to be the light of the world, the Church is that congregation of those who, as yet, can only imperfectly express our true identity as the sons and daughters of God. So may our prayer of this week bear fruit through us in sharing a greater attention to the light that shines in Jesus Christ, who is perfectly united to the Father in the Holy Spirit and in whom we apprehend the unity that is splendour with no bounds.

Beatific Theology

Feast of St Thomas Aquinas
Westcott House Chapel
John 16.12–15

DR JEFF PHILLIPS

A teacher who had a profound influence on me was fond of saying that all the best saints were local. He believed that there was a kind of continuity between the lives of the saints, great and small, and the canon of the Scriptures. He thought a great deal about lives like those of Dietrich Bonhoeffer, Martin Luther King and Dorothy Day and of what it meant that these lives, and others less widely known, were unintelligible apart from the gospel. Regardless of the flaws, foibles and failings of people, influence great or small, there is something about these lives that is compelling, attractive and reveals to us something important about the Way we are all trying to follow.

What might it mean for us to take Thomas Aquinas as a local saint: this Doctor of the Church whose work stood on the altar along with the Bible at Vatican I? How are we to take Thomas of all people as a local saint? His work has been put to so many varied and dubious uses and has famously been used to sponsor some ugly things. I think it is fair to say that Thomas would be horrified by this reality. And he would be especially dismayed by one of the basic mistakes that underlies all of these instances: using his work as a bludgeon rather than the starting point of reasoned encounter.

Perhaps the starting point is to ask the question: what are you doing here? This seems to be an ongoing question for people doing theological education everywhere. And actually a question for anyone who, seeking to be formed in the Christian life, thinks and reads about God.

One of the persistent worries for some concerns the usefulness of theology for ministry as for life. A worry for others concerns the perception that what you learn in ministry courses doesn't seem up to scratch, and is a little shallow. We can all think of people who fulfil the stereotypes: 'I don't want to learn theology: I want to help people.' 'I really wish that they had taught us how to do the account books and things like that while training, there are books for the theology.' And there is of course that performative contradiction – the arrogant or narcissistic theologian (or theology student) – those who think you will never be any good as a priest unless you know what they know.

These two poles seem to be universal in Western theological education: egotistical and arid versus air-headed. Or more charitably perhaps, the practitioner versus the theoretician. Both of these are surely ditches to be avoided. But how then are we to think about what we are doing? What is theology? What are we doing here?

You could say that these are not poles but two sides of the same narcissistic coin. To say that the subject of theology is God, as Thomas insists, may not be the obvious redundancy it first appears to be. For we are amazingly good at turning ourselves into the subject of theology. Which can be fine too, as long as we embrace ourselves through God. Theology is not narcissistic, but beatific. What does this mean? Let us see if our hero can give us a tip or two.

For all of the multiple uses and identities drawn out of Thomas's most well-known work, the *Summa Theologiae*, it was first a formation manual written for a group of insurgent social radicals whose life together was about engaging with common people and the poor, as well as the most challenging intellectual questions being addressed in the early universities, which were already convulsed by intellectual revolution. That time and its questions still profoundly mark our own.

One of the important things to remember about the thrust of Thomas's thought, crafted in such a context, is the first word of his famous hymn: *Adoro te devote*. Adoro, 'I adore', is probably the closest to an on-the-ground epistemological principle we have got. One of his followers, Nicholas of Cusa, would say that your loving is your seeing, and modern cognitive science would seem to bear this out. What we pay attention to and are attracted by forms our world, our habits, and dominates our time.

'Adoro' is connected to one of Thomas's other central insights, that because God is the creator and source of all things, reason and faith are crowned by glory. There are no such things as non-graced moments in creation because creation itself is God's grace. We are held in being by God without being overwhelmed or overruled, but we are attracted by one sense of 'good' or another. For Thomas, grace is participation in the divine nature. And our created natures are not destroyed, but crowned by grace and glorified. 'Grace is the gift of God and the gift of participation in God, because what grace does – what God does in us – is deify.' Habits (those things formed in us and given by God through the Holy Spirit) are not only those of virtue, but also practices that define the community, namely sacraments; the first brings the divine life formally, so that we become like God, the second (sacraments) effectively, so that the humanity of Christ works in us. As in the humanity of Christ, so in his members; in grace the Holy Spirit does not bypass but 'rests upon and shines out from the body'.[12]

Thus for Thomas, theology is about God, not in some sort of simply conceptual or formally propositional sense: it is about us being drawn into the divine life, perfected, deified, gloried. We are drawn by the goodness of this beatific vision.

So again, how are we to answer our question: what are you doing here? I would like to think that Thomas might say that you are embracing another step of being transformed from one degree of glory to another, journeying ever deeper into the divine life that is larger than any of the narrow agendas of theology or 'churchy-ness' as we often understand it.

This time is about gaining new vision, and habits that connect to and deepen your attraction to God who led you here in the first place. This is the work of God the Holy Spirit. But as Thomas was fond of pointing out, God is not self-evident in the world because God is not part of the furniture of the world, God is its source. Thus, that this work is often imperceptible to us is as it should be because God's action through the Holy Spirit is not like one billiard ball smacking another, it is about our natures being perfected and drawn into the divine life, not being overwhelmed or destroyed by it.

So direct all that you do here to the object of your adoration, be patient with yourselves and the fact that you can't see all that is happening to you. Make room for the idea that perhaps what is going on is your own perfection, your very being drawn into the divine life, your nature being infused with grace even in the midst of times of perplexity and grief.

We encounter tonight in our Gospel disciples who could scarcely assimilate the fact that Jesus was actually taking leave of them. This remarkable journey with the most compelling person they had ever met was ending. They are insensate with grief. But the thing that is even more difficult for them to take on board, is the immensity of the goodness that was about to be bestowed on them: namely the divine life itself as they have seen it at work in Jesus through the Spirit. Perhaps the word from Thomas, our local saint, is that we too in this particular context are being formed by a divine pedagogy whose object is deification. If so, it is wise to buckle up: it can be a bumpy ride being formed by the love that moves the planets. We must continually hold fast and know that being formed by the goodness of the gospel requires endurance, in the knowledge that your nature is being crowned by grace and finding its fulfilment in glory. And this glory that rests on the God-Man we will see repeated in the lives of others and in countless other ways, drawing us ever deeper and propelling us on.

Out of the Dark Time

Presentation of Christ
Southwell Minster
Malachi 3.1–5; Hebrews 2.14–end; Luke 2.22–40

JOHN MILBANK

Today is a festival of light, but darkness is much on our minds. When I wander into the bright Sicilian café in Southwell I often encounter Geoff, a member of this congregation, reminding yet another person that the Vikings used to name this part of the year 'the dark time'. And this part of the world can sometimes still seem part of the gloomier Danelaw of pre-conquest and pagan times, especially when the fog in the Trent valley is so bad that you can hardly see ten feet away from you. But transferring our thoughts from the Midlands to what the Saxons called Middle-earth itself, the whole world, the word 'dark' seems also much in the air. Are we returning to dark times and is that because we have too much ignored the darkness already gathering all around us? And are we now too much tempted towards drastic, dark solutions in an increasingly threatening and incomprehensible contemporary reality?

In the face of all this, it would be tempting to say that Candlemas simply offers a message of contrasting light and hope. It is true indeed that today we return from January to Christmas, with Epiphany framed by the last story of Christ's babyhood. And to some degree, the cold secular January, when our minds fast-forward in despair to the thought of summer holidays, is what we get and what we deserve if we forget that Christmas and Epiphany are all one continuous arrival and manifestation of God in the world. Our English ancestors kept their halls and cottages festooned right up till this festival; but nowadays we are too worried about the mess and the smell of rotting leaves.

But on the other hand, the January descent into darkness after Christmas may not be wholly inappropriate, in symbolic terms. For Candlemas is not just a welcome reminder of the seasonal good news of Christ's coming and showing-forth to our physical reality. It is that indeed, but it also sounds some significant dark notes, which are only apparent if we think closely about the tale told in today's Gospel.

It is, above all, a story about the Jewish Temple. The Temple in the Israel of this time was the centre of cults about the end of the world and a final arrival of God in glory. That was because the Temple itself was seen as a focus of divine presence, often understood in terms of God's female indwelling as Wisdom or Sophia, intimately arising from the earth. It was often expected that God would finally show himself as an angel in the Temple and would arrive to purge it, in the way spoken of by the prophet Malachi in our reading. A fully true worship of God would then at last be possible and the priesthood itself would be purified, in words that usually make English people hear the music of Handel in his *Messiah*. But the bright promise of his musical setting is not inappropriate, since while Malachi speaks of a coming of judgement, this is a purging that will render us all, priests and laity, more our true selves.

And it is this positive day of glory to which Simeon and Anna, the Temple servants, are shown as looking forwards. Their role was liturgical, and indeed Simeon's Nunc Dimittis song in our reading has become a cornerstone of Christian worship. But their future expectation was of a tremendous, colourful event, very much Handel-plus, full of the sound of trumpets, with a messianic angel wielding a triumphant sword. A very fine scholar from Nottinghamshire, the Methodist Margaret Barker, has pointed out that Anna is said to be the daughter of Phanuel: no personage in the Old Testament, but one of the archangels in the apocalyptic book of *Enoch*. If Anna's human father was named after this figure, it suggests still more her devotion to a Temple-cult of expectation. There are also reasons to believe, as Barker argues, that her name 'Anna' links her to traditions about the restoration to the Temple of the sacred tree, the tree of life itself of the Garden of Eden. Anna may have been a high priestess of the tree, again a sign of the presence of God in the world as wisdom.

The important role of female figures in this story relates yet more strongly to the figure of Mary, our patroness here at Southwell Minster. She is brought to the Temple, like any Jewish woman, to be purified of blood-contagion after the birth of her child; she is identified as a poor woman because she is only expected to offer the sin-offering of two turtle-doves or pigeons, not a whole-offering or holocaust also. And yet Luke oddly and obscurely seems to conflate her purification with the presentation of her baby Jesus, in terms and words that clearly suggest he is offered as a sacrifice. But did Mary, who had given birth, according to the tradition, without pain through the Holy Spirit, really need to be restored from the alienation attendant upon childbirth to normal social intercourse?

We have surviving hints here as to a complexity surrounding this question. In our Christian past, dramas and popular sermons often drew upon the extra-canonical infancy Gospels, like that of James. In this account, Mary was identified as being, like Isaac in the Old Testament, the late miracle child of another Anna (significantly) and her husband Joachim, and was offered by them to the Temple as a gift. There she lived we are told until she was 12; she danced on the Temple steps and later helped to weave a new veil for the Temple in colours of purple and red. When she reached puberty, she was seen as impure and had to leave, but Joseph was appointed her guardian and, after the miraculously pure birth of Jesus, had to return her to the temple.

It is this very moment that is also recounted by Luke. There is an intimacy between Mary and the Temple because she is figuratively herself Israel and Jerusalem. In the various messianic prophecies, this mother figure was usually also present, as in Isaiah. She also is to arrive in the renewed future. Indeed, to invoke the sound of Mendelssohn, the Sun of righteousness who is to arise 'with healing in his wings' just a bit later in Malachi 4.2, is female in Hebrew and it is without question really 'her wings'. The new dawn of Christ is not possible without the assent given to his coming by Israel in the person of Mary.

How then is this glorious story also a bit chilling? Well, normally, in a process to which Luke alludes, any Jewish firstborn son has to be bought back from God for the price of five shekels. Otherwise, the suspended fate of Isaac, about to be offered to God by his father Abraham, still hovers over their heads. But in this case no such transfer is reported by Luke as being made. How could it be, since for God incarnate there can be no equivalent price? But that means that the blow removed from Isaac has now fallen on Jesus. Why has he been brought to the Temple at all, if not to be offered as a sacrifice?

In this way, the story of the Son repeats that of the Mother. Jesus and Mary are intimately linked with each other as both belonging to the Temple, as Temple offerings. Indeed, the strange identification of a girl child with Isaac made by James is fearfully confirmed when we learn that a sword is going to pierce Mary's heart also. As in the case of her son, the blow is no longer suspended over her head but is really going to fall.

No arriving angels, drums and trumpets then. No unification of Israel under God. Instead, what Luke 2.34 calls a 'sign of contradiction' with some to rise and others to fall in a divided nation. If we then today are tempted to think that pure nationalism is the dark answer to darkness, then the Gospel writer does not agree.

The good news, the in-breaking of light, is rather that the sign of contradiction will now reach the Gentiles, all of Middle-earth, even the Danelaw Midlands, once the Christian King Alfred has done his work.

But what is the contradiction? It is twofold: first, evil is not at root a sinful breaking of the law but an impossible denial of reality, an impossible wound to the heart of God. Second, this denial of God impossibly implies the death of God, an impossible putting of God himself at risk. But in realizing that God is a universal trans-cosmic God who is brought into the world by his contradictory suffering of our wrongs, not a national God distantly offended by the breaking of particular ethnic laws, however admirable in intent, we at last see in this darkness the true light.

Thus, the universal breaks through – but in the fragile human shapes of a specifically and locally Jewish mother and child who turn out to be infinitely more than all nations and civilizations. In Christ we see God himself, suffering unto death on our behalf that he and we may live again. Seeing him through Mary we understand how we can receive this death and share in it in order that we may also live. As the Church, the Marian spouse of Christ, we have become the new Israel, which name was taken to mean 'those who see God'. But he is now seen in a wholly new way.

The role of Mary and of ourselves seems passive and secondary, but in a way, it is not. For just as Christ could only arrive through the manifestation of divine wisdom already in Mary's assent, so too Christ can only be reborn in a dark world today through the assent of Christ's bride, the Church, to his constant and universal re-arrival. May light now shine out of the darkness in East Mercia and everywhere this coming year.

III

Unfolding the Story:
Lent to Easter Sunday

The season of Lent is prefaced now with the Feast of the Transfiguration: a revelation of his glory is set before our gaze, before many churches veil their crosses and prepare for a fast of the eyes. To help people really inhabit sacred time, Lent must be as dramatically different as possible from the preceding season. Lent is a time to face sin directly as an existential reality in a way that does not leave people feeling guilty, but that offers them a sense of being taken seriously, and offers the hope of forgiveness and transformation. The struggles of our Lord with the devil in the wilderness open an understanding of our own lives as ones of meaningful spiritual warfare. Lent is also the time when people come together in study and prayer groups, when preaching enables the deepening of attention by the whole congregation.

Passiontide marks a turn towards Jerusalem and the cross, and must involve meditation on the atonement mystery. To a Patristically influenced vision, the important element in such a proclamation is an emphasis on the notes of victory over sin and death. This is to avoid forensic and legalistic accounts of atonement and stress our own participation in the passion, death and resurrection of Jesus. Preaching in Passiontide and Triduum is aimed at opening the story to our own inclusion, paralleling the double-edged mimesis of the liturgy of Holy Week, through which both join in the Palm Sunday hosannas, and, in the dramatic Passion reading, cry for Jesus' death with the baying crowd.

Traditionally, the three days leading to Easter Day were thought of as one, which reveals the deep truth of their unity. While preaching has a liturgical tact, maintaining the dramatic structure of the days, because Christ already reigns from the cross even the events of his mocking, death and burial become the territory of proffered joy and victory.

On Being Dust

Ash Wednesday
Christ Chapel, Episcopal Theological Seminary of the
Southwest
Isaiah 58.1–12; 2 Corinthians 5.20b–6.10;
Matthew 6.1–6, 16–21

Dr Anthony D. Baker

Some critics have argued that Isaiah in fact has three authors, and that the book can therefore be divided into three sections. Here is my shorthand summary of their messages:

First Isaiah. The people are walking in darkness.

Second Isaiah. The people walking in darkness have seen a great light.

Third Isaiah. The people walking in darkness saw the light, but it turns out not to have been quite as bright as they'd anticipated.

So why do we need a third Isaiah? Wouldn't it have been more hopeful to let the second author have the last word?

Early on in Isaiah, with the Northern Kingdom doomed to exile, the prophet warns the Southern Kingdom that her sins too will find her out, and her day of doom and exile will soon be at hand. And then 39 chapters and perhaps 200 years later, after Judah has, in fact, fallen, there comes the unfathomable moment of grace. Now Babylon has fallen to a foreign king, and the poets of Judah can remove their harps from the willow branches by the river and come back home. This celebration concludes with the unforgettable image of the welcome home party that knows no end: mountains will burst into song when Judah walks by, the trees will stand and applaud, and peace will reign in God's holy land.

But then there is a third beginning, and it carries us through today's reading: 'Announce to my people their rebellion, their pretentious fasts, their lack of faith.' What happened to the bio-cosmic curtain call? Why are we back to judgement and repentance? If the second Isaiah ends in eternal blossoming of myrtle and cypress, why do we need a third?

A possible answer is that the later readers of the prophet needed to know who they were supposed to be in the story. Given the choice, I'm sure they'd have preferred to stay with that bit where the trees clap their hands (however that's done). But the fact is they were stumbling their way back into old habits, the sorts of prideful faithlessness that had been the occasion of that original dramatic calling of the cranky prophet in the first place. They are measured and found wanting, which means, as the prophet had said way back in the year that King Uzziah died, that they stand in danger of being uprooted. What's uprooted has no hope of staying alive, save in the unlikely event of the desert bursting forth with springs of water – which in fact happens in chapter 41. So, when these mid-Second Temple Jews stand with an eye on the bliss of Second Isaiah, and both the ears bombarded with the new judgements of Third Isaiah, it's as if they've been shuttled like a pinball all the way around to the beginning of First Isaiah, and called to repentance all over again.

We begin a similar return to the beginning today. Ash Wednesday is a day of contradictions. On no day is it more evident that the last will be first, and the one who loses her life will save it. And, of course, the day that Jesus preaches on hygiene is the only day that we get our faces dirty on purpose.

I'll tell you what I want, more than anything else in the world: I want Easter. I want the mountains to sing and the rocks to cry out, the dead to rise, the trees to clap their hands, and the cypresses and blue bonnets to burst into bloom. And Isaiah tells me the same thing the church calendar tells me year in and year out: I can't have Easter. I stand here with one eye on the eternal and cosmic procession of joy and peace, wondering how I measure up, and I hear the words spoken to me this morning, and the text messes with my head: 'Shout loud, do not hold back.' This sounds good: the mountains and hills are going to burst into praise around me; it's the Easter of restoration for me, I just know it – 'Lift up your voice like a trumpet' – angels play trumpets all the time: now they're going to join all the earthly creation in welcoming me into the peaceable Kingdom! And then the dagger: 'Lift up your voice like a trumpet, announce to the people their rebellion, to the house of Jacob their sins.' And just like that, I'm whisked back under the 39 chapters of judgement, where I am reminded over again, in so many ways, that I am a man of unclean lips, and I dwell among a people of unclean lips – no offence meant to the present company, of course.

Easter evades us, because people with unclean lips don't get to look the God of Hosts in the face. The problem here is that we've got such a short memory. We were baptized into the exile of Christ's death and the miraculous restoration of the resurrection, and sealed as Christ's own for ever. That ought to engrain our name in us pretty deeply. That should send us straight to Easter morning. But we've been offered other names along the way: 'Be the one who lusts for power and prestige. Be the one who is disloyal to those who trust you. Be the one who refuses companionship. Be the one who prefers bitterness to reconciliation. This is who you are.' These names are offered to us, just as new names were offered to Christ by the Tempter; he refused, we accept. We believe in sin, rather than believing in our baptism. We accept the Tempter's names because it's easier than believing in the one given to us in baptism. To believe in pride, and even to believe in despair, is easier than to trust in God's mercy and grace.

And so, when the joyous procession leaves for Jerusalem, we find ourselves still weeping in Babylon. When the fog has lifted outside Christ's tomb, we find that they've taken our Lord away, and we know not where.

But there is grace hidden in the withdrawal of Easter, just as there is grace hidden in the messianic overtones toward the end of today's Isaiah reading: the broken walls will be rebuilt. Today we are told the deep and mysterious secret of our true identity: you are not who the Tempter tells you you are. You are not your disloyalty, you are not your lust, you are not your wretchedness. It's much better than that: you are dust. Dust that was shapeless, lifeless, nameless. Dust that once upon a time could neither sin nor love. And God breathed on the dust, and it became a living, loving soul. That's who you are: nothing but dust ... dust touched by the breath of God. It's good to be dust. And thus, as Isaiah says, will the dry garden flourish, will the ancient ruins be restored, will the broken walls be rebuilt, will the barren sands of the desert rejoice in the miracle of water. Only as we acknowledge and bewail the drought, the ruins, the brokenness that we ourselves are, will we be healed. Not by a heroic refusal of penitence, not by a heroic act of self-willed transformation, but only on our knees.

So be dust. For 40 days, while the kiss of Easter withdraws from our unclean lips, remember who you are. Fast, repent, cast off the false names that you have believed in far too long. And then, perhaps, we will pass together through the 40 days and 39 chapters of the curses and threats and judgements, even through a dark Friday and Saturday night of death and loss and exile weeks from now, to a miraculous morning when new shouts will come to us – come to us while we weep by the rivers of Babylon, and invite us to sing the songs of Zion with the mountains and hills and all of creation: 'Christ is risen!'

But for today, and tomorrow, and the day after that, let's be dust. That way, in the quiet posture of penitence, we'll be ready to hear a whisper, ever so faint, that will sustain us through these 40 days: 'Remember that you are dust.' Oh, it's good to be dust. Because the life that blows through this dust is the life of God, and the love that ignites this dust is the love of God, and the grace that covers this dust from head to toe is the grace of God. It's good to be dust. Thanks be to God, it's good to be dust.

Living in the Rhythm of Worship

Sidmouth Parish Church
Exodus 17.1–7; Romans 5.1–11; John 4.5–42

THE REVD PREBENDARY DR DAVID MOSS

What is worship? What are we doing at this moment, gathered in this place and progressing through these motions and movements: sitting, standing, singing, listening, giving, receiving, eating, drinking, kneeling? What are we up to? If an alien walked through the doors of this church at this very moment – and for so many in our society they are effectively aliens to the experience of worship – I wonder what they would make of this event? What would we have to tell them of what we are doing?

Like some of you I expect, it was a pleasure and a privilege to be in this church for the nearby College's carol service just before Christmas. But it was also interesting – perhaps even a little sad – to see just how 'all at sea' so many people were with corporate acts of singing or silence, to name but two of the building blocks of worship. Now this is no more a judgemental observation than it is a covert encouragement to you to lend a helping hand to any visitor who seems unsure. It is simply to point out how, 'below' the language of our liturgies, there lies a still deeper stratum of expression: a level of 'motions and movements' that we can no longer presume to be the common inheritance of every person who is drawn into this church – neither the movement itself nor its intelligible meaning.

So, I wonder where you would begin to explain what you're

67

up to in doing this thing called worshipping? Would you start somewhere about the same place as that Samaritan woman in the gospel story: our ancestors have always done this thing called worshipping in this certain place, whether it be mountain or church. It's just the sort of thing you do. Or would you perhaps begin by describing a thirst you found within yourself a long time ago; a thirst that in some strange way is quenched in bread and wine, Word and water; and in being quenched, so, mysteriously, is the thirst deepened?

As I look at your faces I wonder what you would answer? For in answering this you will be laying bare much of what you understand your Christian journey to be about: its trials and its joys, its disasters and its hopes. In one way or another you have learnt and tasted the mystery of the One who promises eternal life. And you have responded, as the Samaritans before you: 'we know that this is truly the Saviour of the world'. You have lived in and through worship – and as the world seems to speed past us, never forget that this is a great gift and a great grace, and your task will always remain, as best you can, to pass this experience on.

But it is not easy – perhaps you know this in many ways better than I do. It is not easy to pass on this skill, this passion, this obedience to worship. And not only is it not easy to pass it on to a world which is so thirsty for sensation and satiation; but, increasingly, I wonder whether it's getting more difficult to pass this on in a Church concerned to make God present to ourselves in sensation and satisfaction, rather than allowing the rhythm and shape of worship itself to draw us into the sacrificial presence of the One who alone might save us.

So then worship of the Christ – the one who declares himself to be the Messiah to the Samaritan woman of all people, as his disciples exclaim – what is this worship that we must reckon with here? What is this strange thing – worshipping the Father as Jesus says – that is to be pursued in Spirit and Truth?

I want to say two things about it which, I hope, will in some way touch your experience, and your thirst to worship – however strange it may seem. Worship has to do with a rhythm and with signs – and for both of these we depend utterly and joyfully upon our God whom we must worship in Spirit and Truth.

Why rhythm? Jesus in St John's Gospel, in interpreting Moses' act of lifting up the fiery serpent in the wilderness, declares: 'No one has ascended into heaven except the one who descended from heaven, the Son of man' (John 3.13). And just because he has ascended so we may thither follow – we proclaim. The rhythm of God's gracious 'down-beat' in coming to us as man is now to be met in the 'up-beat' of the One, Christ, who in ascending to the heavens has returned us to the Way that leads back to God. Up-beat and down-beat: this is the rhythm of worship. We worship in the 'up-beat' – of aspiration, hope, desire, thirst – because we have heard and received the 'down-beat' of God's gracious desire and thirst seeking us out and resonating throughout our lives. It is a note sounding from all eternity to which we now give answer. We now know how to pitch our response because the Christ has struck it for us. And so, we must always listen and wait upon his word.

Just so: 'A Samaritan woman came to draw water', to lower her bucket deep into the heart of creation to find the gift of water so that she may draw it out. Down-beat/up-beat. And beside her stands the Christ asking to drink – in other words explaining to her – a Samaritan woman who is doubly distant from what is proper and acceptable – the sign of water. Through the rhythm of reaching down and lifting up, we are to discover signs to show us the Way.

We have to listen and learn and follow the rhythm of God in our worship if we would have it be worship of *God*, and not something else; that is, just listening to ourselves. But now it appears we are to listen, and learn and follow this rhythm through signs. Signs like water, signs like the doubly disreputable Samaritan woman, and above all the sign of the Son of Man lifted up so that the world may be saved.

However, it may be that this story of the Samaritan woman at Jacob's well leaves us wondering: signs and the stuff of the world – is this really necessary for worship? After all Jesus himself says to the woman in response to her question about the proper venue of worship (the mountain or Jerusalem): 'But the hour is coming, and is now here, when the true worshippers will worship the Father in spirit and truth.' Now in the language of St John's Gospel to worship 'in spirit and truth' does not mean worshipping in a wholly interior or mental way, but worshipping according to the rhythm of the Holy Spirit given by the Father after the resurrection.

But still does it not make us wonder a little? To worship the Father do we have to have all these signs and rites, these sacraments that unfold in more or less obligatory ways, making use of antiquated gestures and movements, of pre-programmed formulas? Does all this in fact run counter to the true rhythm and spirit of a free-flowing spontaneous worship – worship that doesn't need all this encumbrance of church? Many times, I have heard people say to me: you don't need to go to church to worship God. And there is a deep truth in this for sure; and it is one that every thoughtful Christian who has felt the thirst to worship will probably have wrestled with in some way or another in their lives.

However, when this sense of the true freedom of the Spirit, unconstrained and blowing where it will, has caught our hearts and minds, so also is it the case that from the very first, from its origins, the Church has responded to the wind of the Spirit in seeking the truth of God through ordered prayer, shapely worship and the sacraments: in particular, Baptism and the Eucharist. And why? Because the pulsing rhythm of God's life coming down to his creation and gathering it up to return it above comes to reside in a fully human being – a body, somebody, Jesus Christ: And Jesus said to the Samaritan woman, 'I am he [the Messiah] the one who is speaking to you.'

In Christ, the rhythm of God's life, which is boundless love, is literally bodied forth – this is the meaning of the incarnation. And the Word became flesh and dwelt among us. But if this is so, then for Christian faith, for Christian worship, its deepest secret is this. What is most spiritual, and most divine, always takes place in what is most corporeal, and most bodily.

Worshipping according to Spirit and Truth is learning through life-long patience, attention and struggle to discover the freedom of God in the ordered life of the body of Christ, the Church, so that this life may be discovered wherever the Spirit leads us far and wide.

God and Nature

University Church of St Mary the Virgin, Oxford
Genesis 1

The Revd Dr David Neaum

I have a confession to start with – I find more moderate forms of
secular humanism at times quite attractive. It was once said about
John Austin Baker's much loved book, *The Foolishness of God*, that
half the attraction of reading it was that you never knew whether
he was going to throw in the towel and renounce his faith. Sadly, for
you this sermon isn't going to be quite like that, but I think what I
find attractive about the humanism of someone like Philip Kitcher
is the honesty with which he responds to his scepticism about the
claims of religion and his attempts nonetheless to find a moral
framework in the wake of his rejection of God. As an ex-chorister,
he has an appreciation of Christianity that perhaps tempers his
critique away from the anger of the New Atheists, but this means
he can't be as easily dismissed as merely destroying straw men.

Christianity needs to be able to respond seriously rather than
dismissively to these critiques, for in some ways the humanism
represented is more tolerant and attractive than the narrow
and exclusive literalism of some Christians. However, secular
humanism and biblical literalism are in fact strange counterparts
to one another and responding to one involves responding to both.
What Kitcher and other secular humanists reject above all is the
notion of transcendence – rightly pointing out that the term is as
vague as it is prevalent.

In light of this, one of the questions I find myself returning to is how do I articulate belief in God and faith in Jesus Christ in ways that acknowledge God's transcendence and yet do not insist that God's involvement within the world must abrogate what we understand of the natural world, human history and social development.

Within the Christian tradition, the idea of God's transcendence ultimately comes from two places: the first is found in the experiences that many people have had throughout the ages of something more, something beyond the material that gives of itself to manifest something about the way things really are. The second is the account of creation in Genesis. This doesn't require a literal reading of the creation story, but neither does it neglect its poetic beauty or theological richness. Instead, it focuses on the underlying theological idea that the spatio-temporal universal is fundamentally dependent for its origination and continuation on something beyond it – something transcendent – to which we give the name God. We can say then that the Bible – in this case the mythopoetic but also theological text of Genesis – has revealed something about the way things are, articulating our sense that there is something more in terms of a transcendent, creator God.

The idea of transcendence is fundamental to Christianity, but while Genesis might give theological impetus to the idea, philosophy allows us to draw out its significance. When we think of God within the Christian tradition our imaginations tend towards some form of personalization – God as Father or as Son, God as speaking or acting or willing – and rightly so. But behind these personal terms by which we relate to God lies the idea that God is the source and ground of existence itself; that the essence of all existent things lies beyond them – transcends them. This is the idea that there is a fundamental difference between the essence of things and their existence – between what they are and that they are. For those of you whose eyes haven't rolled back in your heads yet and who care: this is old school metaphysics but not the onto-theology critiqued by postmodernism, for this difference is an ontological difference between Being itself and existent beings. God, as Being itself, is radically transcendent to the spatio-temporal order.

This philosophical articulation of a theological, indeed scriptural, understanding of reality is where the real difference between secularism and Christianity can be found. Christianity gives voice to all those who have had an intimation of something more, something beyond, that gives significance to reality and to their lives. Secularism expresses the refusal of this possibility in favour of an horizon of meaning delimited by the material world and our own conceptualizations of it.

For the secularist, we are alone in the universe and when the lights go out it is dark. For the Christian, we are always sharing in something greater than us, discerning and cooperating with it or resisting and obscuring it. When the lights go out for us as individuals they continue to shine, augmented by what we have contributed or diminished by what we have obscured.

But let us put philosophy aside and ask: 'how do we know that God who is utterly transcendent?' And the answer, perhaps unsurprisingly, is through revelation. But there is a difficulty here exemplified in the different approaches of the secular humanist on the one hand and the biblical literalist on the other. Secular humanists think that the natural triumphs over God and thereby denies revelation. They hold that the natural is all there is and so a transcendent God must be denied and the Bible relegated to mere myth or fiction. On the other hand, biblical literalists think that God triumphs over the natural and reveals himself by doing so. They think in effect that God is all there is, for the natural world can be abrogated by God's will.

To get beyond this false opposition, we need a different account of the relationship between transcendence and immanence – between God and the natural world. We find it in the very idea of God's incarnation. In the incarnation, the transcendent God is immanent in a natural human life without being mixed up or confused. Without losing the emphasis upon God's transcendence, the writings of the New Testament testify to a God who is revealed in, and as the self-imparting gift of, love: in and as a relationship between a Father and Son.

The incarnation is the event that makes sense of everything else. The long history of human discernment of God or of Israel's relationship to the one unknowable and un-nameable God, finally reach their fulfilment in the incarnation. What is revealed in Jesus Christ is that the very relationships we enter into as human beings can reveal something of the self-imparting gift of love that is the very Being of God. Despite everything, our human nature can participate in the divine nature – our love can share in God's love; who we are is analogous to who God IS. We are relational beings and God is revealed as a relationship of love between the Father and the Son in and through the Spirit. When we share in God's love we share in God's Spirit.

This is of course only a theological sketch, an outline, but of one of the most important issues in contemporary theology. I wanted to try and give you a sense, however inadequately, of how the critique of secular humanism might be met and that the dialectic between secular humanism and biblical literalism can be overcome from within faith. The natural does not need to triumph over or banish God. Neither does God need to triumph over the natural to be revealed as Love. God is revealed in and through the natural – through human relationships and the ways in which we understand them. Jesus Christ reveals that the transcendent God's very Being is a relationship of love: love that in Christ is fully and materially present and yet always exceeds that materiality through love for the transcendent God known and related to as Father. This love is what we are invited to share in as Christians, and I commend it to you as the very essence of who you are and are called to be.

A Wondrous Exchange

Passion Sunday
St Bene't's Church, Cambridge
John 12.20–33

THE REVD RACHEL GREENE

Today the Church enters the final two weeks in this Season of Lent. From this point onwards the liturgy focuses our attention on Jesus' passion and death. A number of theories have developed over the centuries in an effort to make sense of the saving work that God did through Christ to reconcile the world to himself. They are theories of the atonement. Here the word 'atonement' denotes the reconciliation of parties that had been estranged, so that the two are now 'at-one'. Atonement theories are concerned with how we are made at one with the One who gives us life. For at the heart of the Christian faith is the assertion that Jesus suffered and went to his death not just as an individual but as a representative of us. As our representative, he died for us, taking upon himself the guilt of our sin and in some mysterious way dealing with it and disposing of it; and thereby liberating us to live out the new future he has secured for us.

Theories of atonement wrestle with the logic and mechanics of what Jesus did on the cross, in light of what Jesus taught the disciples about his death before (and after) it happened and in light of their experiences of receiving God's forgiveness and God's Spirit. Despite the depth of faithful thought here, I find most atonement theories unpalatable. The way the atonement is sometimes explained, humankind has offended God by disobeying his commandments, and in so doing offended against God's infinite dignity. To make restitution or satisfaction for the offence was impossible for any except God's Son, who obediently gave his sinless life to provide the infinite satisfaction required, therefore restoring the relation of sinners to God. This theory is known as Satisfaction Theory, but I seriously doubt that explanation would satisfy anyone today.

Another way the atonement sometimes gets explained is that Jesus restores the relation of sinners to God by suffering on our behalf the penalty of condemnation that we deserved, thereby appeasing God's demand for punishment. This theory of Substitution and variations on it, suggest a God who can only be appeased by the shedding of blood, but who is prepared to accept the blood of his Son in place of the blood of us all. While that explanation might make you feel grateful to Jesus, it ought to make you extremely wary of his heavenly Father. Personally, I recoil at the idea of placating a wrathful God who demands bloodshed, a twisted justification for violence if ever there was one. And I'm disturbed by the suggestion that God the Father did something to God the Son, perpetrating some sort of divine child abuse.

But then I came across an astonishing prayer, which has been instrumental in changing the way I think about the atonement. The prayer was reportedly discovered on an inner wall of a Nazi concentration camp. It goes like this:

O Lord, when I shall come with glory into your kingdom, do not remember only the men of good will; remember also the men of evil. May they be remembered not only for their acts of cruelty in this camp ... but balance against their cruelty the fruits we have reaped under the stress and in the pain: the comradeship, the courage, the greatness of heart, the humility and patience which have become part of our lives because we have suffered at their hands. May the memory of us not be a nightmare to them when they stand in judgement. May all that we have suffered be acceptable to you as a ransom for them.

And then the prayer concluded: 'unless a grain of wheat fall into the ground and die ...'.

I find the prayer extraordinary. Here are irreparably damaged people asking that the harm done to them be forgiven and transformed. 'May the memory of us not be a nightmare to them when they stand in judgement.' And what is even more striking: that the harm done to them would be a ransom for the perpetrators of this violence. 'May all that we have suffered be acceptable to you as a ransom for them.' This is a prayer of people who have taken up a role in God's redemption of their oppressors, and who offer up themselves in love to that end. It is a curious exchange – the prayer beseeches God to reap the benefits of their torment in the form of a harvest of virtues they'd acquired by undergoing that suffering and then to credit those benefits against the debt of the transgressors. They propose 'a wondrous exchange' – to borrow the language that the Church Fathers like to use. The image of exchange offers another way of thinking about the atonement.

What if the incarnate Son of God became what *we* are, so that *we* might become what we are meant to be: sons and daughters of God? Let me put it another way, what if Christ descended for us, experiencing our sorrows and bearing our burdens, in order for us to ascend to him and share in the *joy* of divine life? What if, in the words of Gregory of Nazianzus: '[Christ] assumed the worse that he might give us the better'?[13]

This language of exchange doesn't get us into the mechanics or details of how Christ's suffering atoned for the sins of the world, but I think it shows why Jesus' atonement amounts to more than providing satisfaction to God or sparing others the punishment they deserved – and that is because in these exchanges there is a very strong statement of solidarity. That assertion of solidarity runs all the way through the accounts of Jesus' life and death presented in the Gospels. Over and over again we see Jesus lined up with those who are sinned against – victims of every sort of injustice, discrimination and abuse. But Jesus does not just align himself with victims. He also aligns himself with victimizers, and offers the same self-surrendering love to them that he offers to the blameless. Perhaps that is why reflecting on Christ's atonement can be so unsettling. It reminds us of not our own vulnerability – bringing to mind the ways we've been sinned against – but it also calls us up to face up to our own culpability – the ways we, as sinners, are implicated in oppressing others. It also begs some important questions: how far are you willing to extend forgiveness? Where does love or pity for those who know themselves to be guilty come to a stop in your life? What would it take to push you past that place?

The great Catholic novelist George Bernanos was once visiting some monks when he read in the newspaper about the arrest of a mass murderer. Bernanos was so upset by what he read in the article that he sent a letter to the man's lawyer. In the letter, he says: '[the situation] is heart-rending in that there is in it a hope that one can scarcely conceive of: the solidarity of all men in Christ...' Bernanos continues, 'As far as I am concerned I have nothing much to offer him. [But] I would like him to be able to understand that there are monks ... who do better than just pity him, but who will from now on take over, as brothers should, part of his appalling burden.'[14]

When Jesus atones for us on the cross, he does not just die for our sins. According to the logic of exchange he also raises us to his nature, and he does so not merely by imputing the results won onto us but by giving us a share in his mission. For that reason, you and I have a role to play in God's work of healing, reconciliation and mercy, along with all those who show us how to make the sacrifice. We too can extend God's forgiveness to those who need it most. We too can lift the weight of each other's burdens. It only depends on this: whether we who owe our lives to God, can let them go ... for the sake of the Harvest.

'I tell you, unless a grain of wheat falls into the earth and dies, it remains just a single grain; but if it dies, it bears much fruit.' (John 12.24)

Inside the Story

Palm Sunday
St Michael and All Angels, Bedford Park
Mark 10.46—11.10

THE REVD DR MELANIE MARSHALL

When you're in the story, you don't know how the story ends. The disciples don't understand how their king can be least among them and servant of all. The crowd doesn't understand that this king will triumph over death itself. To them he will simply suffer death. The High Priest. Pontius Pilate. The imperial soldiers. They don't understand how anyone can be a king without an army. It is the blind man, Bartimaeus, who sees: that the Son of David is the one we look to, in our vulnerability, for healing. But even his eyes have been opened to see the one who saved him only to behold him scourged, and disgraced, and executed.

None of these know the end of the story. But we do. We know that there will be defeat, and also that there will be resurrection. When we hail Jesus, do we hail him as they did? As the one who will give us what we want, what we expect? Or do we know that to follow Jesus is to enter into a story: a story of loss and confusion, a story that contains many bitter chapters before the promised resurrection? A story of dogged faith, in which our heart's desire will come to us; but not in the ways we demand or fantasize about. Not as a series of triumphs. Our heart's desire will come out of confusion and disappointment. It will emerge, dawning on us, out of dashed hopes.

Except for the Lord himself, no one in this story knows the

ending. They can only see in part. Now, they see before them their king, their saviour. But then, something goes wrong. Then, he is arrested. Then, he is tried. Then, he is a failure. Then, he is a disappointment. Then, they are embarrassed that they ever believed in him. Then, they are angry that he has let them down. Then, he may as well be dead, so much rubbish, because he is not the thing they wanted him to be.

God is not the thing we want him to be. God is not going to follow our plans, and slot in with our expectations. There will be death, and there will also be resurrection. That is our advantage: the advantage of knowing the end of the story. We can't always see the end of our own story when we are in it. We can't avoid pain and disappointment. But we know at least that our dashed hopes are not the last word. That when our expectations are confounded, it's because they were expectations as limited and faulty as we are. The resurrection reminds us that what we want for ourselves – a king! A Messiah! A saviour! A magic trick to make it all better! – is not where our salvation lies. When you know the end of the story, you know something the crowds don't: that when we lose our hopes, it is because God has planned something infinitely better. Better than we can ever ask, or imagine.

If the Christ had been everything the crowds expected, this story would end with a dead king. Because the Christ was so much more than the crowds expected, the story ends with a risen Saviour. Unconquerable, dragging death itself in chains: death itself the defeated enemy.

Who, as they lined the streets to cheer him, could have hoped that the Lord would fulfil his promises of a Messiah in this manner? In a manner so strange, and so rich, and so cosmically and eternally transforming? Blessed is he who comes in the name of the Lord. Hosanna in the highest heaven.

Food Enough to Triumph

Maundy Thursday
Episcopal Church of the Incarnation, Dallas, Texas
Exodus 12.1–14a; Psalm 78.14–25; 1 Corinthians 11.23–26;
  Luke 22.14–30

So mortals ate the bread of angels; he provided for them food
enough. (Ps. 78.25)

I have a good friend from college who is a poet. Ed Madden grew
up on a farm in Arkansas and his family has a tradition at the time
of the burial of a family member. The funeral home digs the grave,
but the whole family fills in the grave with dirt. They talk and tell
stories about their deceased loved one as they shovel the dirt into
its place, as the body is returned to the dust. In a poem about the
burial of Ed's aunt, *Watermelon*, the burial is interrupted, when
one of the nephews recalls the watermelons that used to 'mark off
the days / with sweet irregularity':

> We have only to grasp
> the rail that flanks
> the coffin, lift it, gently,
> carry it, slowly, from the front
> of the church
> to the hearse humming outside.
> The funeral has been well planned–
> the hymns she chose last spring,

the shovels Henry has waiting
in a pickup near the grave.
What is not planned
is the watermelon.
The watermelon Henry requests,
retrieved from the nearby shop,
and the pale blue cooler of cokes;
my brother and I return
to the shed blazers and the vivid wilt
of silk dresses, return,
our arms full of grace:
the chunks of pink sugar,
the sweet juice, wet seeds
and rinds like green
jewels on the cemetery lawn.

Ed and his family eat and work and tell their stories about his aunt, renewing their sense of family and community.

Tonight, in the reading from Exodus, we hear another story. Though this story is of the founding of a nation, it is not so different from the story that Ed tells. Before the Exodus, Israel is a loose band of tribes. That first Passover night, they became a Nation and they are told to repeat this feast yearly. It is to be their narrative, their story.

The Feast of Passover marks the night when the angel of death passes through the midst of Egypt. Death is to wipe out beast and human alike. This plague turns Pharaoh's heart and convinces him to release the people of Israel. It is a triumphal moment for Israel. But it is a moment full of fear. They are told to be ready to leave in haste. They eat unleavened bread, because there is not time to let the dough rise. They eat this Passover meal with their running shoes on, their loins girded for a journey. They are about to make a break for it. Their fear is thick; children crying, women and men rushing around to prepare for a mass exodus from what had been their homes for all of their lives. Tyranny and death stand just beyond the door. Dare you go out that door!

And yet they are commanded by God to eat. Why? Who could

eat at such a moment? Part of the flight-or-fight mechanism of the body is the rush of adrenalin. It makes you feel nauseated. It makes you sick to your stomach. And they are commanded to eat and they are to eat every last bit of the bread and every last bit of the lamb. There should be no leftovers in the morning because in the morning they are going to be on the run for their lives. And if they get away from Egypt, the trials of the desert await them. Death lurks just outside the door, just beyond that next hill. Death lurks in the Red Sea, and it lurks just beyond that sea in the desert. It is ever present for them; it is actually ever present for us; we just manage to ignore it.

Arthur C. McGill, a Canadian theologian, wrote a book called *Death and Life: An American Theology*. In that little book, McGill offers a scathing critique of American views on death. He says that we worship what we fear and we fear death; in that sense, we worship death. He says that we hide from the little 'd' deaths: we fear grey hair so we buy Grecian formula; we fear wrinkles so we get surgery to tuck them away; we fear pale skin, which looks so much like death, so we have tanning salons on every corner. According to McGill these are just the symptoms of our fear of Death with a big 'D'. We try to drive it away, to hide it, to put it from our sight. We create technology to save ourselves from it and we create a whole industry to take the dead body away from our sight. We cannot bear to see death; we want to dress it up cosmetically so that it does not look like death. We want to have machines keep us alive. Technology will be our saviour. Oh, if it were that simple. We actually only hide death with our technology.

Imagine for a moment that you are in that upper room at Jesus' last Passover. That night is not so different from the night some thousand years earlier in Egypt. Do not picture the scene as depicted so famously by Leonardo da Vinci. I do not think that image captures the truth of the moment. I do not think it was that calm or that serene. Rather, the disciples are scared to death. If you remember they did not want to go up to Jerusalem on Palm Sunday. They fear going into Jerusalem. They are afraid of what might happen and the scene that Jesus made at the Temple earlier that week did not help one bit. They fear capture. They fear death. They are fishermen without much standing in the community, not a lick of political sense – except for Judas, perhaps. They could be sacrificed and no one would care. They are a bunch of crusty old fishermen, a boy – John – and a traitor. Everything that goes bump in the night sent a chill of fear through their spines. None of them could have been very comfortable.

But they are good Jews and they are not going to miss out on the Passover feast. So they meet in secrecy and they are scared to death that they will be caught this night in this upper room. The possibility of death looms close by on the night of that Passover, the night when tyranny captures the Son of God and when death waits in the wings until noon tomorrow. What anxiety, what nausea is present in that upper room that night.

And then Jesus picks up the unleavened bread and he says the familiar Passover prayers in a way unfamiliar to those people in that upper room. And he blesses the bread and breaks it and gives it to them saying, 'Take; eat, this is my body which is given for you.' And then he takes the cup and blesses it and gives it to them saying, 'This is my blood of the new covenant.' Today those fearful men and boys become a new people. They would become a community of believers and though they all, save one, will lose their lives for that Church, they take that new story and they run with it. The Passover story has changed; that night it became their story … Tonight, it is our story. It is retold this night and every Sunday because it forms us; it is who we become.

And of all cultures and societies that need the story of this night, it is ours. Death looms just beneath our technological denials. It was real that night of the first Passover; it was real the night Jesus was arrested; it was real on that hot Arkansas summer day on Ed's family farm; it is real this night. We have hidden it away with our technology, but it is still there. And what are we to do in the face of death? We are to tell our story and we are to eat. We are to re-tell that story of our founding, the story of our salvation. All of our personal stories make sense in light of this story. The story of this night is not just a story that breaks the grip of political tyranny. It is a story that breaks the grip of death itself.

We are to stand at this altar – at this table – and we are to eat. Tomorrow death will triumph for a time, but tonight we eat. The bread and wine are Life. The body and blood are our sustenance. With this food, we affirm that we will live in the face of death. This food mocks death; this body and this blood destroy death. This food is our salvation; Jesus will be our Saviour. *So we mortals will again this night eat the bread of angels; he provides for us food enough to triumph.*

Passionate Actions

Good Friday Three Hours
Southwell Minster

THE REVD DR ALISON MILBANK

In his meditations for the time we spend in prayer in commemoration of Christ's three hours on the cross, John Muddiman chose instead of the traditional seven words seven actions that figure in Matthew's passion narrative. In so doing, he recalled to the congregation that the earliest passion narrative most probably emerged in the first century after Christ as proclamation, a text precisely to accompany the ritual actions of the liturgical restaging of the Lord's Supper. We present here just two of these actions: the anointing at Bethany and the offering of the sponge on the cross. In the original liturgical context, the reflections would have been joined by appropriate prayers and hymns.

The Anointing at Bethany (Matt. 26.6–13)

The passion narrative opens with this scene, and its importance is underlined in the last verse: wherever in all the world the gospel is preached, this act will be remembered. Just the act, nothing else. Even the woman's name has been forgotten because she poured her whole identity into this one beautiful thing.

It was not an unthinking act of extravagance performed in a rush of enthusiasm. If it were, the disciples' complaint would have been justified: the perfume should have been sold and the proceeds given to the poor. What altered the character of the action in this case and changed it into an enduring symbol was that collectedness and deliberation which attended it. Slow motion was a technique developed by an Austrian priest in 1904: running a camera at a higher speed, then playing it back at the normal speed of 24 frames a second, you see things normally invisible: the corona made by a drop of water in a puddle, for example. Here, when the gesture is seen in slow motion, its deeper meaning is given time to register. The poor can applaud it, for they understand the gesture. They recognize in Jesus their own special representative and champion who, by his poverty, enriches them.

The liturgical act of anointing is connected in Scripture with the appointment of Israelite kings and priests and this provides the immediate background for the woman's action. She fulfils the role of a prophet, coming into the room where the men are eating and officially consecrating the Messiah. Jesus was under suspicion as a claimant to messiahship, yet so far nothing had been done to justify that accusation except a rather ambiguous ride into Jerusalem seated on a donkey and surrounded by a happy crowd. There had been no stage-managed ceremony of anointing in the desert as with other messianic pretenders. But at the very moment when the authorities were deciding to proceed against him in any case, the conclusive proof they needed was actually occurring under their very noses in Bethany. But this was no pretence; it was a genuine royal and priestly anointing. By it the counterfeit King of the Jews, Herod, and the illegitimate High Priest, Caiaphas, mere creatures of a foreign power, were toppled and usurped.

This is the immediate background to the meaning of the act of anointing, but into the foreground comes a new idea, which Old Testament precedents do not contemplate. As the first official act of his reign, this Messiah is destined to suffer, to die and to be buried. 'She has anointed my body in advance for burial,' Jesus commented. It had to be done in advance for when other women arrive on the first Easter morning to complete the Messiah's lying in state, God will have anticipated them by anointing him as his Son for ever with the Spirit of holiness by raising him from the dead.

This passage, then, combines the idea that Jesus is our rightful King and High Priest with the idea of his humility even to death on the cross. There is power here but it is not coercive power or domination, it is rather the power of self-giving love.

One final comment on this first scene. We often speak of the death of Christ as a sacrifice. It is always a huge paradox to call the crucifixion itself a sacrifice. The public execution of a condemned criminal is the exact opposite – an unholy, defiling death. A sacrifice by contrast is a sacred immolation, the ritual slaughter of an unblemished animal in the Temple. When we use this language, then, we are flying in the face of the facts of the case, and employing only one part of the metaphor. Jesus' death is a holy and deliberate act, despite appearances to the contrary. Other aspects of the metaphor are less appropriate, especially the idea that God could ever demand such a sacrifice.

But this woman's action is an unmistakable instance of sacrifice in the literal sense. Her breaking the neck of that veined alabaster jar and pouring its whole contents over Jesus' head was a costly, self-conscious act of devotion to God of something which was at her disposal and therefore could be completely surrendered. This sacrifice may help us to pinpoint the sacrificial element in that other act on the cross. The breaking of the veined vessel of the body of Christ and the pouring out of his life-blood and spirit in deliberate self-offering and consecration to the will of God. In a plainer sense, sacrifice is what we do in response to the passion – what we offer to God through and in Christ. As St Paul says, 'We are the aroma of Christ to God among those who are being saved, a fragrance from life to life,' like the perfume that suffused the home of Simon in Bethany.

In our silent meditation, let us try to visualize this act of anointing. Let the perfume of the woman's sacrifice fill our senses and inspire us to wonder and gratitude that we have in Christ, a King who was humble even to death, a Priest who consecrated his will to the Father, a Messiah who reigns through the power of love and reveals to us the character of God.

The offering and drinking of the sponge of vinegar (Mark 15.33–39)

The cup of suffering that Jesus had long anticipated is now presented for him to drink. He had prayed in the garden for it to pass him by but had vowed to accept it, if necessary, as God's will. And here it is actually presented to him. It turns out to be not a cup at all; it cannot be delicately sipped. It is a sponge full of vinegar stuck on a pole and squashed into his face – a drink he cannot refuse.

This act was not performed out of kindness, but out of curiosity. The drink he was offered here was not a drug, wine mixed with myrrh to dull the senses, which he had earlier declined. It was a stimulant forcibly administered to keep him alive just a little bit longer. Some of the bystanders had half-heard him calling on Elijah, or so they thought. They thought that if he did not die too soon they might actually see Elijah swoop down from heaven to rescue him. Their curiosity was aroused. So this terminal act of symbolism turns out to be just as ironic as the others we have considered. The cup of suffering becomes a sponge of vinegar designed to drag the proceedings out as long as possible. But God mercifully shortened the day. After the sponge, Jesus gave a loud cry and breathed his last.

The irony of this scene, the administration of the communion cup, is not limited to the symbolic action. The irony spills over to the only word from the cross recorded in the passion narrative of Mark and Matthew: 'My God, my God, why hast thou forsaken me?' These were the words misheard as a cry of help to Elijah. They were in reality, an urgent appeal to God his Father, a quotation from the first verse of Psalm 22, which goes on to describe with uncanny accuracy the trauma of crucifixion. That psalm ends on a note of hope and deliverance, but it is difficult to suppose that Jesus began here to recite it in full. No, he chose these precise words because they fitted his immediate situation, and he shouted them in a strangled cry.

But what do they mean? Neither the action nor the saying seem to speak of communion, but rather of desperate alienation.

What was Jesus alienated from then? From God? That is hardly possible if he was one with God in heart and mind. What does this forsaking refer to? Modern people tend to think of this sort of thing in psychological terms – that Jesus no longer subjectively felt God to be present to him, that his inner vision had become clouded in despair. But in the original psalm and in many other places in Scripture, being forsaken by God is understood not psychologically but physiologically. It is a very objective forsaking. Death is separation from life and thus also separation from God, the source of life. Death is the point in the journey of life at which God finally leaves us. For it is the Spirit of God that we feel now in our bodies. He is closer to us than the air we breathe. If there is any hope beyond death, it is not to be found in us, but only in God who, in his mercy and faithfulness, may gather up the broken pieces and recreate the conditions we need for life. Our existence, whether in this world or the next, is always dependent upon God. This is the Jewish and Christian doctrine of creation.

Jesus cried, therefore, 'My God, my God, why have you forsaken me,' *why am I dying*? It is a cry of loss, certainly, of falling away from God into nothingness. But it is not loss of faith, or loss of love for God. It is the cry of a loss of life; for life is communion with God and death is forsakenness.

Jesus's words remain therefore a genuine prayer, and appeal to God to be 'My God' even as his basic gift is being withdrawn. Jesus gathered up all the diffused pain of his bodily suffering, and concentrated it into a single point, so narrow that no theory of the atonement could be based upon it, but so sharp that it penetrates to the heart of our experience of communion with God even at the moment of losing it.

In its context therefore, the final symbol, the cup of suffering that turned out to be a sponge of vinegar, can indeed be seen as the cup of communion. For God is our life and he alone remains when life itself abandons us to death. Let us meditate on the action of offering the sponge and see it fulfilled in the cup of communion with God, the author of our life and our sole resource in death.

Death's Name for Love is Resurrection

Easter Sunday
St Margaret's Anglican Church, Winnipeg, Canada
John 20.1–18

THE REVD DR DAVID WIDDICOMBE

'Christian preachers have always faced the problem that what is most existentially critical to their message is least credible to their hearers.'[15] Or, put another way, Christian preachers have always had the advantage that what is least credible to their hearers is most existentially relevant to their actual situation. That is to say, that while the resurrection is what is least credible to their hearers, it is in fact the only known solution to their fundamental problem – death.

As Mary Magdalene knew full well, death is fatal. Human life reliably, inevitably and irrevocably ends in death and death is reliably, inexorably, universally fatal. Death is a tomb from which there can be no escape, the Kingdom from which there is no return. Death is in fact a scandal beyond comprehension. Death means that the human race, nay, that life itself has lost the battle of survival. That death will live and reign supreme and have dominion over all, and life will be as if it never was, and perhaps should never have been.

Mary Magdalene knew beyond any shadow of a doubt that Jesus was dead. She came while it was still night. She entered into the black portal that leads to annihilation, she was in the midnight garden of good and evil, she closed upon the tomb, she entered the kingdom of death. Jesus was not there.

What does this mean, that Jesus was not there? A recent headline announced that some Christians are modifying their doctrine of the resurrection. Does this mean that they are modifying their doctrine of death? What could modification mean, except that we have decided to negotiate a better deal with death? That we have agreed to resist it a little less vigorously? That for some slight concessions, we will grant the main point? For the main point will have to be granted and in truth it is the only point. Death is death and death is final.

Certainly, there are some minor points of history and of theology concerning the resurrection that might be debated. But they are minor. The big issue is clear. There is no point in trying to fudge it. In fact, since in our culture most people already don't go to church, don't want to go to church, probably never will go to church, there is little point in telling them that we have modified the one thing that might have made it worth their while to come in the first place.

This would be as if a major pharmaceutical company was to run an ad saying that they had developed an exciting new drug: it won't cure cancer but is otherwise pleasant enough, relatively harmless, and not overly expensive. Without the resurrection, without the bodily resurrection of Jesus from the dead, that is all that Christianity is: just another religion. Pleasant enough, relatively harmless and not too expensive, but it does not do anything that would make it worth the effort to get out of bed on a Sunday morning. Don't bother trying to sell that to your neighbour.

You cannot negotiate with death. And Mary Magdalene didn't try. One minute she expected to find a corpse, and the next she was holding on to Jesus, clinging to him, in love again with a living, breathing Lord. It was not the result of meditation, discussion, negotiation, or wishful thinking. She did not go running breathless to the disciples to tell them that she had found herself clinging to an idea about the immortality of the soul or reincarnation or about the beloved living on in blessed memory.

The point is this: she didn't find her soul filled with peace, she found the tomb emptied of its corpse; she didn't find her head wrapped around a new idea, she found her arms wrapped around her Lord. 'We were anxious about the soul', says Augustine in Sermon 261, 'and he by rising again gave us assurance even about the flesh.'

It is just that simple. Nobody claims, probably no serious person has ever claimed, that this is easy to believe. In fact, the Church claims it is not. That is the whole blessed point, that in Jesus Christ God has made a direct, frontal and an altogether successful assault upon death. That God in Jesus Christ also outflanked death on the right and on the left. And that in Jesus Christ he carried out an altogether successful attack in the rear. That God in Jesus Christ has defeated the final enemy. That God in Jesus Christ, quite frankly, has done the one thing necessary, which was the one thing necessary just because it was the one thing impossible, the thing that had never been done before.

Just as death has us so comprehensively surrounded and cut off, so the gospel announces that God has surrounded and cut off death. The whole point here is that it is just this simple, comprehensive and incredible. And that is why believing it ought to be called by its ancient name, which is Hope.

I am not asking you to believe it, though many of you do. I am inviting you to hope for something. It is like news to a beleaguered city. The enemy's main army has been defeated, utterly and completely defeated and driven from the field of battle. Help is on its way. You may not believe it, but only a fool would not hope it. That is to say, we live by hope. We have heard news of salvation.

To the scientist who said that we know that there is no life after death, Wendell Berry has wisely replied that we know no such thing. Nor do we know that there is. We live, he says, by hope. Jews and Christians live by hope in the resurrection of the body and hold God to make good on his promise.

Historically, the Church has been resistant to any suggestion that it modify its shocking central claim, to give up its hope for the sake of something more believable but far less useful. For as Augustine said: 'the resurrection of the Lord Jesus Christ is the distinctive mark of the Christian faith'. As Luther said, there is nothing to preach about except that Jesus Christ says in effect, I am risen from the dead and have overcome and taken away all sin and all misery. Now you may be worried that you don't have this kind of hope. But remember that hope is hope and not something more, or other.

> Faith is the substance of things hoped for, the evidence of things not seen … Through faith we understand that the worlds were framed by the word of God, so that things which are seen were not made of things which do appear. (Heb. 11.1, 3, AV)

Think of it this way. Had I not seen it with my own eyes, I would not have believed the reports that I was about to be born. I would have said it was entirely unlikely, miraculous at best. I would not have been able to conceive of my own conception. Why is it that we conceive both children and ideas? Where do they come from? They are miracles. For her part, Mary Magdalene would not have been troubled if you had said to her that you did not believe her report. Neither did Peter and John, exactly. They went to check it out. John believed what he saw but nothing is said about what Peter thought and in any case, they did no more about it than you are going to do after this service. They just went home.

So what it comes down to is this. Either death is love's defeater or love will overcome even death because love is only known to death as resurrection.

And this morning there is only one thing to do about the resurrection. Whether you believe it, half believe it, or only hope that it might be true, the best thing to do is to celebrate and sing about it and name it in all its glory. One thing we know for sure: Mary Magdalene didn't believe it until she saw it, and our state of belief or unbelief does not matter much to her. She knows in whose nail-imprinted hands we are and she trusts him more than she trusts us, for she trusts us to him.

And so, on this resurrection morning, we might understand how a poet might know more than he knew he knew and might even have spoken from the heart of Mary Magdalene when he walked into a church and heard the sweetest voice whisper to his soul, 'I don't need to be forgiven for loving you so much.' Leonard Cohen has it right. It *is* written in the Scriptures and it is written there in blood. And it is true that the angels declared it, not from above but at the empty tomb. Indeed, from death's perspective, 'there ain't no cure for love'. Death's name for Love is resurrection.

IV

Real Resurrection:
Eastertide to Trinity Sunday

For a radically orthodox charism, Easter is the occasion to declare the resurrection as a mystery, but a true mystery, that breaks down all our mental compartments in which physical and spiritual, heaven and earth, death and life, are blown away. Incarnation, redemption and resurrection are, in a sense, one event, in which God's love takes us through physical life and death to the only life possible beyond it, which is in him. Resurrection, then, is not a tacked-on happy ending, but the logic of God's love for the whole cosmos. To put it paradoxically, our fulfilment as human creatures is supernatural.

Another focus that arises from this faith in the resurrection is the impossibility of any part of life that can be called secular. As the Orthodox theologian Sergei Bulgakov argues, the world has become a great grail or chalice, holding within it the bodily fluids that fell from Christ's body on the cross. And resurrection opens to the horizon of the *eschaton*, when all will be gathered up and our true humanity revealed in one and the same moment as we see Christ in his full glory. Worship, which lifts us to the heavenly liturgy, anticipates this fulfilment, and preaching, as part of worship, shares this eschatological function. The upward symbolism of the Ascension is not something for which we should awkwardly apologize, but celebrate, for we are all indeed 'heaven-bent'.

A creedal emphasis in preaching also has a high view of the Trinitarian feast day, which completes our journey into the life of God. This is a not a dry doctrine but the goal and medium of our participation in the divine life. It marks out, Pope Emeritus Benedict argues, 'what is revolutionary about the Christian view of the world and of God ... that it learns to understand the "absolute" as absolute "relatedness".[16] Trinity Sunday properly follows on from Pentecost, in which the gift of the Holy Spirit itself reveals the nature of the Trinitarian life of God, and mediates it to us. For a radically orthodox perspective, the Spirit is thus the revelation of God's love and its mediation. She allows us to discover the divine activity in the world and acknowledge it to be good, without accommodating to secular interpretations.

Disturbing Faith

Evensong, Jesus College Chapel, Cambridge
Genesis 32.23–33; John 20.24–29

DR RUTH JACKSON

The other disciples therefore said unto him, We have seen the Lord. But he said unto them, Except I shall see in his hands the print of the nails, and put my finger into the print of the nails, *and thrust my hand into his side*, I will not believe. (John 20.25, AV)

Except I thrust my hand into his side – how are we to fathom Thomas's extreme and grotesque demand? Unwilling to believe that the crucified Jesus has actually returned, alive, to meet with his disciples, Thomas asserts that only the opportunity to probe Jesus' raw and open wounds will be enough to convince him.

Perhaps, if we treat Thomas as a measured and scientific doubter, we can defend him on the grounds that his demands are surely proportionate to the leap of assent he's been asked to make. Why indeed *should* he believe, without precedent and without proof, that a man he knows to have died so violently has now been raised to new life, and in bodily form, too!

It's not clear, however, that Thomas's disbelief does – or even could – match such a scientific and dispassionate standard. We don't know much about Thomas from John's Gospel, but in the two places where he does speak, his lines betray a simple yet ardent devotion to Jesus. What Thomas does, we gather, is to follow Jesus, and what he desires is to be alongside him. And so when the other disciples tell Thomas that *in his absence* they have seen the Lord, Thomas does not simply face the task of processing the 'idea' of bodily resurrection. Rather, what he has thrust upon him is the prospect that there may be things about Jesus that he cannot understand, things inaccessible to him. If these other disciples are right, then has he not been denied the opportunity to be with Jesus again? Excluded from a group in the most distressing of ways? All of these thoroughly human considerations – grief, shock, the prospect of exclusion – seem to crowd in on Thomas's extraordinary demand for proof.

For the other disciples, John tells us, it was enough to *see* Christ's hands and side in order to believe. And even if simply seeing Christ would not do, then why does Thomas demand to probe Jesus' nail prints, and feel inside Jesus' spear wounds? Would it not be enough to grasp hold of the risen Jesus – to be comforted by the warmth and solidity of his arm, his shoulder, or even his face? A little earlier in the chapter, how does Jesus react to Mary Magdalene's desire for contact? 'Do not touch me!', he exclaims to Mary 'because I have not yet ascended to the Father' (John 20.17). Now that Jesus has declared it taboo for Mary simply to make contact with his body, Thomas's subsequent stipulation about interrogating Jesus' flesh appears even more extreme. I struggle to fathom what Thomas's demands can tell us.

One thing they do give us is a striking impression of how Thomas pictures the resurrected Jesus. By demanding to grope and to handle, rather than simply to see, Thomas is envisaging, and indeed emphasizing, the bodily character of Jesus' risen life. These stipulations repel the idea that the risen Christ is a spirit – however realistic-looking – or a ghost. His demands place front and centre the fact that Jesus has suffered an agonizing death: that Jesus' body bore nails at its extremities, and a spear through its side. Thomas envisages that such marks, such sufferings, have not been wiped out in Jesus' resurrection glory. For Thomas, the risen Word *still* takes on flesh.

Imagined within Caravaggio's 1602 painting, *The Incredulity of Thomas*, is the very physicality suggested in Thomas's demand for proof. We see a lean, smooth, Jesus on the left, and a ruddier and rougher-looking Thomas opposite him, his profile front and centre, and then two further disciples are drawn in, peering over from the back. But it's only Jesus' bared body and hands – and Thomas's right hand too, of course – that's properly visible here: this flesh is the focus of the painting. Otherwise, the image is of four huddled heads, choreographed together like the four points of a diamond, or even of a cross.

Highlighting the grim detail of Thomas's grubby thumbnail, Caravaggio has Jesus grip Thomas's wrist firmly, in order to guide his thick finger into the folds of his own flesh wound. Jesus' skin is pushed apart and puckered by Thomas. Caravaggio, exploring the literally disturbing nature of this moment, thus also draws us back to Christ's suffering on the cross.

When, eight days after Thomas's outburst, the disciples meet again, this time Thomas is with them. Jesus arrives – having confounded physics, locked doors, and walls – and having greeted his disciples with his peace, he then turns to Thomas, and offers him precisely what he had demanded: 'Reach out here with your finger', Jesus says, 'and see my hands; and reach out your hand, and thrust it into my side.' 'Do not doubt', Jesus implores, 'but believe' (John 20.27).

Jesus *says* this to Thomas, then – he confronts him with this frightening offer: '*put your hand in my side*'. If we were to go with Caravaggio's painting, then we would assume the next line in the Gospel would note that Thomas went ahead and *did just this*. But in fact, and as Glenn Most has remarked, the text gives us no such explicit detail. What Thomas did or did not do here remains, in effect, an open question: could he bring himself to touch Christ's wounds? Did the horror – the profound intimacy – involved in this act catch up with him, as he faced the prospect of it? All we're told for certain is Thomas's immediate verbal reply, which communicates the shock of his recognition: his astonishment as he realizes who he's facing. 'My Lord and my God!' Thomas answers.

Thomas's story begins by speaking of a fleshy resurrection. But in this moment where the text is silent about what Thomas actually does when he's face to face with Jesus, in this moment his story opens up and out to invoke the glorious transcendence of the risen Christ. Now he has seen, Thomas believes. Now that he has seen, he realizes the limits of his knowledge, the limits of his expectations. He finds himself surprised beyond measure: he finds himself face to face with his God.

Thomas's position is thereby turned on its head in John's Gospel – from doubting and demanding proofs, to being confronted and shaken by an astounding revelation.

Before he is able to believe, Thomas must see. But this 'seeing' we speak of is not merely the seeing of an object, a wound, a proof. Before Thomas can believe, his very presumptions and expectations must be blown apart. He assumes that he will be the one to judge – that he will be the one to doubt or to assent. And yet, when Thomas finally comes to faith, this faith that is demanded of him comes from outside – it is given to him in the jolt of his recognition. 'My Lord and my God!'

From Thomas, therefore, we learn about the transformation of human longing. From him we learn how faith in the resurrection cannot simply mean faith in *continuity*, or in a return of the same. Faith is not a holding out for what we once had, and want to have again. Instead, Thomas has it forced upon him that resurrection means *new creation*, it means radical discontinuity, surprise, the *un*known.

The master Caravaggio manages to signal Thomas's transformation: Thomas's ultimate passivity in this story, despite his original active protests. I've already pointed to the strong guiding hand of Jesus in the image. Thomas can probe because his hand is pushed: he submits to Christ's own pressures. Thomas's lined forehead is thickly scored by the depth of the thought-tracks running across it. Yet when opposed to the brows of the other disciples, which appear strained and interrogative – furrowed because of *examining* eyes – Thomas's forehead seems to be creased in astonishment; he is wide-eyed. *He cannot believe his eyes*, we might say.

And so if we are to take something from Thomas, perhaps we can take this: that we leave ourselves open to surprise; that in faith we should expect to have our expectations blown apart. For as Jesus' words run at the end of John, chapter 20: 'Blessed are those who have not seen and yet have come to believe.'

Being Witnesses

Third Sunday of Easter
St Mary Magdalen's, Oxford
Luke 24.35–48

THE REVD CANON DR PETER GROVES

You are witnesses of these things. (Luke 24.48)

Christian teaching is essentially clear. Christian teaching is also essentially mysterious. These two statements do not contradict one another, because a proper understanding of mystery will leave us in no doubt that there are some truths – truths about God – that cannot, by definition, be understood. I cannot, for example, understand what it means for God to create everything there is out of nothing. Neither can you. You can compare creating with making things, but you will never achieve more than analogical truth, because to conceive of absolutely nothing is impossible for the human mind.

God is essentially mysterious. Talk of God is talk of mystery, not in the sense of a problem to be unravelled, but in the sense of language that takes us beyond the possibility of complete comprehension. But this does not mean that talk of God is unclear. I can make true statements such as 'God became human' perfectly clearly, even though I cannot understand the mystery of the incarnation in the way that I can understand, for example, the economic crisis of the Eurozone.

To say that a statement is clear, however, is not the same as to deny that it is puzzling. Jesus of Nazareth rose from the dead. This is a true statement, and a clear statement, but it is also a puzzling statement, a statement that provokes lots of questions. This puzzlement is something that began with the experiences of those who first witnessed to Jesus' risen life, and some of their puzzlement is addressed by this morning's Gospel.

We need to be aware of what has gone before. In Luke's account, immediately after the extraordinary news that the tomb is empty, we read a detail often passed over in our Easter preaching. The women who have discovered the empty tomb and borne the angels' message back to the disciples are met with incredulity. They told this 'to the apostles. But these words seemed to them an idle tale, and they did not believe them.' The news of the resurrection is entrusted to the women, but the male apostles laugh them out of court. Next we read the story of the road to Emmaus, that marvellous account of pilgrimage in which the presence of Jesus, walking alongside the disciples all the time, is finally known in the sacramental breaking of bread. And it is with the end of that story that our reading this morning begins.

Luke gives us a picture of human fear and doubt being coaxed and reassured by the saving presence of Christ. Now, in this third resurrection tale, after the testimony of the women, after the report from Emmaus, the apostles are ready for Jesus to come among them. Even so, they are slow to respond. They assume they are seeing a ghost. And so, Jesus demonstrates the reality of his resurrection body, showing them his wounds and eating and drinking in front of them. This is someone real, no mere spirit. These actions of Jesus directly address the bafflement, the thorough-going puzzlement, that we would expect in reaction to this boldest of claims – that the one who was known to be dead has risen and is alive.

But that is clearly not the only puzzlement at work here. 'What on earth was going on?', the disciples seem to say by their reaction. For now, Jesus takes them through the Scriptures and the prophets of old, to show that it was necessary that the Messiah should suffer, and rise on the third day. Of course, no straightforward reading of the Old Testament would leave us drawing such a specific conclusion. We might be able to point to individual texts which were seen by the early Christians as pointing towards the resurrection – 'you do not give me up to Sheol, or let your holy one see corruption' in Psalm 16.10, for example, or 'on the third day he will raise us up' in Hosea 6.2. But these are far from representative of the Hebrew Scriptures. What is at work in Luke's account, and in the preaching of the early Church as a whole, is the contention that it is the resurrection that has changed everything, all our presuppositions about what was true. So, the Old Testament, the entire Hebrew Bible, has to be re-read in the light of the experience of Jesus Christ, crucified and risen. All the promises that the God of life has made to his people Israel are now brought to fulfilment for all people in the life, death and resurrection of Jesus.

It is this point – that the resurrection turns on its head all that we thought to be true – which underlies all Christian proclamation and apologetic. That Christ is raised from the dead is clearly true, and clearly mysterious. If we seek evidence for this truth, there will be things we can say, oddities to which we can point, testimonies on which we can rely. But none of these will get to the heart of the mystery of the resurrection, because that heart is nothing other than the risen life of God in Christ, given to you and to me in baptism and renewed in the sacramental life of the Church.

'You are witnesses of these things.' Not only does Jesus reassure the disciples and overcome their doubts, not only does he correct their misapprehensions and redirect their assumptions about the Scriptures they have known all their lives, he ends by telling them that they are witnesses of all that he has been teaching them. It's a remarkably odd thing to say. If someone shows a complete lack of understanding or knowledge of a particular situation, it's strange to provide that knowledge and understanding and then tell them that they are themselves part of the evidence. Jesus doesn't so much say 'look at me', as 'look at yourselves'.

'You are witnesses of these things.' We as Christians proclaim the truth of the resurrection to a world which, many would argue, doesn't want to know. If we seek to prove ourselves right in the argumentative game of power by looking for knock-down proofs and incontrovertible evidence, so that we can best the annoying sceptic who has read too much of the new atheism, then we are just as wrong as our opponents. The truth of the resurrection is not to be deduced; it is there for all to see in the life of grace in the world that God has restored. You witness to the resurrection simply by being here this morning. When, in Luke's Gospel, those women went to the tomb on the third day, they were met with the angel's clear and mysterious question: 'Why do you seek the living among the dead?' Mysterious, because the dead are not expected to be alive. But clear, because what could be more ridiculous than to look for death when what we need is life, to seek the God of life in the one place that God will not be found – in the absence of life and creation that is the tomb.

The life of the Church is the life of the risen body of Christ. As we encounter Christ in the Scriptures and the sacraments we are encountering our true selves, catching a glimpse of the life beyond self and death to which each of us is called. In the Eucharist, we celebrate, we touch the risen Christ and know the truth of his presence with us. And we are witnessing that life – having it revealed to us in Christ, and revealing it to others in all that we do. So, as witnesses to the resurrection, let us take a look at ourselves. Every gift of God, every sign of renewal, every spark of the unexpected, every example of beauty, every act of kindness, every opportunity for good, everyone and everything for whom you are grateful – all these are the manifestations of the risen Christ to which you and I are witnesses. The mystery of the resurrection is clear.

Heaven is Other People

King's College Chapel, Cambridge
Zechariah 8.1–13; Revelation 22.21—22.5

THE REVD DR JEREMY MORRIS

'Hell is other people.' This is probably the most famous quotation from the French philosopher and writer, Jean-Paul Sartre. It comes from a play often translated into English as 'No exit': a vision of Hell in which three people, after their death, are locked in a room where they find, instead of being tortured, that they are expected to torture themselves, by their discovery of each other's desires and failings and living inescapably close to each other. Sartre presumably intends to emphasize the typical existentialist point that our moral choices are ultimately ours alone, and that we have to face responsibility for them alone. But I should think we would all acknowledge some truth in the simple statement that 'Hell is other people'. Families fight, friends fall out, small groups become cliquey and bitchy – time and again. Holidays, with the wrong people, far from being relaxing, can become a torment of irritation and frustration. I personally recall especially two weeks trapped on a canal barge with 12 very different people.

What is it that makes other people so difficult? Is it by any chance that they're not like us – not quiet when we want to be quiet, noisy when we want a bit of privacy, mean about other people we like, or nice about people we can't abide? And that way of seeing it surely doesn't reflect well on us.

But oddly there's a kind of spiritual truth lurking in all this too.

Because other people are a distraction, isn't it true that what we need to do to concentrate on our spiritual needs is, all too often, to find a place apart where we can think and maybe pray? So people go on retreat, usually somewhere quiet, in the countryside, perhaps even a silent retreat. When we pray, we close our eyes to distraction and try to find some inner peace and solitude. When Jesus wanted to pray, so the Gospels tell us, he went out from the crowds, into the wilderness or desert. And you might think then that the paradigmatic form of Christian discipleship is silent contemplation, that all those people who moan like the blazes when children start making a noise in church are right, that silence, inner peace, stillness are the ideal for us, what God calls us to, out of the hubbub of the world.

But I don't think that's the case at all. The model of Christian discipleship ultimately is a party, a great banquet of feasting and merriment. It's in being with others that our true desires will be met, our dreams realized. That's not to rubbish peace and stillness, which we all need from time to time. But we need them in a sense to get some perspective on ourselves in relation to others, so that we can re-engage with the world around us. So it's no accident that we pray for the lonely, the friendless, the misunderstood and abused, the outcast, all those who don't belong in some way to a community or group. We build friendships and families naturally – we're social beings – we can't survive or reproduce without each other, and we know, for it's a cliché really, that almost always human aspirations are fulfilled socially – we're stronger together.

That's why, when the Israelites came to consider the ideal state of humanity, reconciled and fulfilled humanity, there was no better image for them than that of the city. Both of our readings touch on that. The reading from the prophet Zechariah, probably written near the end of the exile in Babylon, foresees a time when God will dwell again with his people in Jerusalem, with the Temple rebuilt. It's not just that the prophet is trying to foretell the future, but he's emphasizing God's providential care for his people, that he will stand by them always, and bring them back – 'I will save my people from the east country and from the west country, and I will bring them to live in Jerusalem', the Lord tells Zechariah.

And in the book of Revelation, John describes a vision of the new heaven and new earth, in which the holy city, Jerusalem, descends from heaven as a city in which there is no need for sun or moon, for its light is the glory of God. When Blake wrote the poem we now know as the hymn, *Jerusalem*, it was that vision of a new city to be built from God's people that he had in mind: and in his hands, of course, it was a social vision, a vision of searing radical egalitarianism, that God will rebuild human relations in a better way than that of the 'dark, satanic mills'. But it is to the glory of God, which is why I never mind having that hymn at weddings or other services, as some clergy do.

This rebuilt, re-imagined city, this city of light and glory, and justice and peace, shouldn't be thought of as pie in the sky. It's not shallow idealism; it's what we're called to reconstruct ourselves, in Christ. We have these readings in Eastertide because they bid us raise our horizon of sensibility beyond the here and now, the preoccupation with celebrating religious truth today, and try to envisage what we might become, in the light of Christ's triumph over evil. Christ is the pattern of our humanity, for John, and in following him and imitating him, in loving others as he did, we simply apply what the resurrection teaches us about overcoming human sin. It's a practical message. We're to recognize our responsibility for each other, and to begin to create the new Jerusalem where we are.

The transformation of our hearts and minds, as we seek to follow Christ, in turn changes our ideas of how and why people fall short and fail, and we come to see ourselves, our own limitations in them. Instead of a sharp, hard line between the 'ins' and 'outs', we can only see a call to everyone to enter the city – whether they respond or not is up to them. John says himself that its gates will never be shut by day – and there will be no night there. The city of God is surely a cosmopolitan place, full of different peoples, races, faiths, a place of festivity, a place of laughter, a place of joy and delight, a place of diversity and acceptance. But it's not a city far in the future. It's a city that exists already, invisibly entwined with the world we're in, wherever Christians try to follow the pattern of love laid down by Jesus Christ. And we can, of course, *make* that city in a sense – we can build it up, we can dig its foundations in our own lives through patient engagement with the needs of the world, not turning ourselves away from others, we can people it with friends and cares, with a concern that takes us out of ourselves, out of our own anxieties and insecurities. And we can begin here, now, in the business of our own lives. Christianity is the great humanitarian philosophy, in which no selfish interest can stand in the way of the love of others. And whatever the Dawkinses of this world say about the metaphysical claims of faith, the truth is that it is not tested in abstract belief, but in practice, in real relationships, in how we treat each other.

Sobering stuff, maybe. It's rather reminiscent of one of Sartre's central points – responsibility. But then it's hardly surprising that many of the great secular philosophical systems of the West have not escaped the ethical framework of the faith that built modern Europe. And yet, Christians should know that all the time what they have to do is to build up the great community of God, the community of common decency and humanity, the community of care. It doesn't matter – in that light – if you don't feel you're a very good, or very convinced, Christian; what matters is whether the love of God dwells in you, and works in you for the good of others. Well, for me, and for all of you, I pray that it may do so.

Love is the Only Politics that Matters

Fifth Sunday of Easter
Hertford College, Oxford
Daniel 6; Matthew 13.1–9, 18–23

THE REVD DR MATTHEW BULLIMORE

Proverbially speaking, politics, like religion, is not a topic for the pub. Nor, indeed, is it always a comfortable subject for the pulpit. But the reading from the book of Daniel interested me because it speaks of politics and of law. And we are, I think it is safe to assert, living in interesting times as far as law and order are concerned.

To help us think a little about the law as it affects King Darius and Daniel, I want to mention a controversial figure called Carl Schmitt. Schmitt was a jurist, a philosopher of law, who was associated with the Nazi party. This fact alone prejudices us towards him and rightly so. His theories of the state seem, however, to have remained in vogue in various philosophical circles ever since the Second World War, and not simply of the right wing.

What has interested intellectuals across the board has been Schmitt's theory of sovereignty, at the heart of which is this: 'sovereign is he who decides the exception.'[17] What does that mean? Schmitt argued that there were times of emergency when the law was under threat from its enemies. There may be forces that would seek to disturb the usual functioning of society, which could not legally be countered. It was thus necessary to suspend the usual working of the law to deal with the threat before reinstating the law. That is, an exception to the law was briefly to be countenanced. Philosophers after Schmitt have suggested that this suspension of the law is actually an intrinsic element of Western legal systems, which usually legislate for their own suspension. The sovereign is the one who decides on the time for the exception, who decides to suspend the law for the sake of the law.

Witness Article 48 of the constitution of the Weimar Republic: it allowed the President to rule by decree without the consent of the Reichstag. On the basis of Article 48, Hitler persuaded Hindenburg to sign the 'Presidential Decree for the Protection of People of State' in 1933, so curtailing various constitutional rights including freedom of opinion, rights of assembly and privacy of communications, and gave the police a right of search and the right to confiscate property. All, of course, under the umbrella of Article 48, which was the legally sanctioned suspension of the law.

Now, we are children of the *24* and *Spooks* generation. But you will know how these TV programmes, in an albeit exaggerated and bombastic fashion, dramatize for us issues of law and order in the contemporary world. Here we see counter terrorists use torture as a matter of course and suspend all usual rules and protocols to achieve the end of saving the law against the terrorist threat. In *Spooks* we see the security forces suspend time and time again what Dr John Hughes would call 'the ancient liberties of the British people'. Today, we even have Hollywood movies about extraordinary rendition. Our world is one in which we all recognize the names Guantanamo, Bagram and Abu Ghraib, names that are synonymous with a stretching of the law to breaking point. Successive Prime Ministers here in Britain have argued for the necessity of the continuance or extension of various curtailments to civil liberty and an increase in security measures.

I think that we can see how the law is being continually revised and even suspended today. It is done to save the law in the light of an enemy who is invisible, whose aims are not obvious, who emerges from the general population unsuspected, who has no obvious political aims or structures and who does not negotiate. It is certainly an enemy difficult to deal with by traditional legal means. The law is doing what Schmitt said the law does, which is to recede in the face of threat. Is it overly polemical to say that today it seems that the thesis that law will always be suspended in order to save the law is being increasingly proven by Western governments in the present climate?

Now, the other interesting thing that Schmitt argued was that 'the metaphysical image that a definite epoch forges of the world has the same structure ... as a form of its political organisation'.[18] We might summarize by saying that all things are related, so the beliefs and ideologies of an era will be reflected in its political thought and practice. Or even better, a people serves what it worships.

So where are we with Daniel? Daniel is the favourite of all King Darius' satraps, his local governors. He is a faithful soul who does his duty and pleases the king but not the other satraps. And so they find fault with him in connection to the 'law of his God'. Going to Darius they present their fears. There are those about who do not live by the law of the land nor worship the sovereign. Perhaps we can hear them whispering, those wily counsellors, that the kingdom could fall if something is not done. Cannot Darius-the-mighty establish an ordinance and enforce an edict that anyone who prays to a God not sanctioned by the state should be executed? You will note that this is not a state of emergency that he will later be able to revoke. According to the higher law of the Medes and Persians, Darius' new exceptional law could not be suspended. The fear of a threat to Darius' divine right to rule, a threat to the religious legitimation of his throne, sends him into a fluster. The law is passed and the threat of death for wrong worship is written into the statute book.

Meanwhile Daniel is on his knees faithfully praying to his God. He is duly arrested and thrown into prison while the cunning advisors tell Darius the bad news. Darius tries to do what he can but he is no longer sovereign; he seems to have lost the power to reverse what he's done. He is in a pretty pickle. What *has* he done? However, as he throws Daniel to the lions, he shouts: 'May your God, whom you faithfully serve, deliver you!' (Dan 6.16). At break of day he hurries to the enclosure and calls out, 'Daniel, servant of the living God, has your God delivered you?' (Dan 6.20). And indeed, because Daniel had trusted God, he has been saved. After a night in what could have been his grave, Daniel rises out of the den to a new life in the kingdom.

The spell is broken and the law that seemed irreversible is revoked overnight, rather like the higher law that saves Narnia's Aslan and vexes the Queen. Darius finds his powers again and deals harshly with his treasonous satraps. Filled with praise for God, he writes to the known world that everyone should worship the God of Daniel, whose Kingdom cannot be destroyed, who delivers and saves, whose dominion has no end.

It is a very Jewish point that is being made and it is repeated in the Scriptures again and again. It is made in different circumstances by Paul in Romans 13.1 when, in stressing obedience to the Roman authorities, he says: 'for there is no authority except from God'. Paul sounds conservative but it is a shot across the bows for Caesar. He is not sovereign, but God, the God of Jesus Christ, is sovereign.

Paul is aware that his Roman friends live in a dangerous world in which the powers that be can wield a sword, where death is their ultimate sanction. And this brings us to the parable of the sower. For there are many seeds that are sown and yet do not survive the perils of the environment. The seed is, of course, the Word. The Word it seems is a vulnerable thing. Persecutions and the lures of the world can cause the Word to be rejected.

The Word was made flesh and yet the world did not accept him and he suffered torture and death. No law was there to save Jesus. As he is passed from the religious authorities to Pilate, Caesar's man, and then on to Herod, the king of his own people, the law refuses to save Jesus. Returned to Pilate and then handed over to the people, Jesus is four times abandoned: by religious law, imperial law, tribal law and democratic law. He dies the death not of a criminal or a prisoner of war but simply of the lost, the abandoned, the nobody. Jesus dies where Daniel was saved. But, to use another seed analogy from the Scriptures, a seed must die to live. Daniel is, for the Christian, a type of Jesus, one who enters the grave and rises out of it to show that no law in the end is sufficient to destroy life, that no sovereign is sovereign over God. The story of Jesus completes what the story of Daniel can only point towards – for in Jesus' death, the ultimate legal sanction – death – is rendered useless because Jesus' resurrection points to something which is beyond the law – the divine law of love.

And what is born from his death? It is the birth of a new community that witnesses to the fact of God's sovereignty by itself incarnating that law of love. The Christian community, the Church, witnesses to the impotence of violence to establish community. The Church is a community in which law is not given pride of place because instead it practises the virtue of peaceableness, it counters violence with forgiveness, it resists futility with hope and faith. If Schmitt was right that the ideological presuppositions of an age structure also the political organization then, in the age of the Spirit, the Church is organized around the founding belief that beyond the law is love, that beyond death is life, that beyond violence is peace and beyond division there is unity.

Is any of this to say that human law is unnecessary? No, it is to say that law is in the end a fragile thing and that it is always at the mercy both of its enemies and also of the fickle sovereigns who can suspend it.

In response to terrorist attacks such as the London bombings of 2007, political leaders sought to increase the 'capacity of communities to resist and reject violent extremism'. The Church confesses to a creed that resists and rejects violent extremism. But the answer it proposes is not a legal one but one that is manifest in the life and death of the one who is love incarnate. If this Word is heard and understood then it 'will bear fruit and yield, in one case a hundredfold, in another 60 and in another 30'.

Let us pray that the love which is sown among us will take root and bear fruit, for in the end that love is the only politics that matters.

The Tangled Vine

Fifth Sunday of Easter
Keble College, Oxford
Acts 8.26–40; John 15.1–8

THE REVD DR JENN STRAWBRIDGE

Then an angel of the Lord said to Philip, 'Get up and go towards
the south to the road that goes down from Jerusalem to Gaza'
[…] So he got up and went. (Acts 8.26)

I think it's fair to say that our readings, and especially the first
reading from Acts, would make any politician facing an election
ballot at the moment rather uncomfortable. Here we have a highly
ranked and respected apostle. He's from the first group selected by
the Church to be ordained as deacon. He's a ground-breaker and
trend-setter; he's serving the people. He's converted thousands;
he's healed the sick: his résumé is awesome. And then the angel of
the Lord sends him away from the capital city, down an obsolete
and rather dangerous road to Gaza. And to make matters worse,
on the road that takes him away from being front and centre, the
Spirit of the Lord sends him to talk to an Ethiopian eunuch, a
potentially transgendered foreigner who is in his constituency.
And they are in the middle of the desert, without a witness or
a journalist to record the encounter. Here, God orchestrates the
most unlikely of relationships that the status quo doesn't permit,
but it's one that leads to the transformation of both a marginalized
individual and this up-and-coming deacon.

But it's not just them. These readings this evening don't sit well with us either: readings about angels and spirits telling people where to go and language of pruning and cutting off. And one of the most uncomfortable themes that runs through all the readings is a distinctive lack of human agency.

The angel of the Lord says to Philip, 'go, go down that obsolete and possibly dangerous road without an end in sight'. And how can you say no to an angel? The spirit of the Lord tells him to speak to the foreigner in the chariot, and, in the heat of the day on said road, he has no choice but to climb in. And then Jesus tells us, I am the vine, *you* are the branches, God is the gardener. Which is all well and good, unless I want to be a tulip or a sunflower. Then what? It's all rather unsatisfactory.

But let's grant, for a moment, the possibility that this gospel might have something to say to us. That this imagery of a vine and branches – even if we'd prefer to be our own kind of flower – might apply to our lives. And the not-so-obvious question is this: if we are stuck as a branch, what kind of branch are you? Now I don't mean are you leafy or fruity or thorny, but think for a moment about a vine and its branches.

Are you the branch who just goes for it, doesn't worry about the other branches, and grows straight out to the side, flourishing and blossoming and doing your own thing until at some point, inevitably, you bend, and even break under the stress of not having much support? Are you the branch that immediately reaches out and grasps onto other branches, pretty sure that you can't grow alone? Are you the branch who is strong enough to allow others to grasp onto you, offering support to those that are weaker and less confident? Are you the branch that stages a coup and takes over all the other branches, grabbing onto any that get in your way and overpowering them with your leaves and your magnificence? Are you the branch that hasn't grown quite yet, for fear of venturing out and showing your true leaves and fruits?

Perhaps there is more choice in how we engage and identify ourselves as branches. For while it doesn't feel like there's a lot of human agency – there simply isn't room in this particular image for sunflowers and daisies – the point isn't about individuality and self-justification but is entirely about community. A community where we begin from a common base – God – a community where we begin with a common vine – Christ – a community where we know that even when we are pruned and life gets hard and uncertain and doesn't go the way we hoped, we are still a part of something bigger.

Moreover, the thing we forget about vines and branches is that they are intertwined: tangled and messy. While we want to be distinct and make sure that, if we have to be a branch, at least we get credit for the fruit we bear, the reality is that our lives are uncomfortably tangled up together. And this is good news, for whether we are in the midst of a moment where we are bearing abundant fruit and really flourishing in our work, our studies, our relationships, whatever it might be; or whether we are in the midst of a moment where we feel a bit cut off, uncertain, unclear about how we fit into the bigger picture, there is a place for all of us on this so-called vine. For this is community. This is Christian community. Although we live in a world that promises we can do all things by ourself, we are reminded in this image, we are reminded by Jesus, that we are dependent on God and on one another. And what a gift that reminder is.

God calls us into community, and like the call of Philip down that road to Gaza and into that chariot with a stranger, we never know exactly what form this will take. Sometimes we will be the loners; sometimes we will be the ones holding up others; sometimes we will be the ones overwhelmed by all the other branches; sometimes we will need a little pruning in order to regroup and re-gather when we break. It's a risky business, this matter of being a branchy community, because it calls us to realize that there is more to this world than our needs and our difficulties: be it an earthquake in Nepal, acts of terror in the Middle East, remembrance of wars past, or acts of violence that call us to respond within our own community. It calls us to shift our perspective to realize we are part of something bigger, messier, and ever changing. And it calls us to be open to God and how we might be surprised along the way, when we find ourselves on a different road from the one we thought we'd be on, or with an unexpected companion, or in an unexpected conversation.

And yet, perhaps especially at *this* time in a world with *these* challenges, these texts are exactly what we need. It's no mistake that the word Jesus uses to describe the relationship between the vine and the many different and disparate branches is 'abide'. A word that has to do with persevering, with persistence, with stamina, with continuing. It's a word we all need this term to give us perspective. Christ calls us, calls you and calls me, to abide. 'Abide in me and I in you,' Jesus says (John 15.4). As the branch cannot bear fruit by itself unless it abides in the vine, neither can you unless you abide in me. Abiding in Christ has everything to do with being part of community, being part of the vine, and of upholding one another, of sitting alongside another in times of flourishing and times of brokenness. And of trusting that when we do this, we are not alone. When we are in trouble, abide. When we are stuck or worried or overwhelmed, abide. When we are at the top of our game and at full strength, abide. For whether on a desert road or on a mountain top, we are called out of ourselves into community. We are called out of ourselves to persevere, to keep plugging away, because we never know if someone right next to us, someone growing near us, might need the support, the strength, the love we might be able to provide when we are enmeshed in community, when we abide and don't give up on the sustaining and unconditional love of God in Christ.

Becoming Heaven-Bent

Feast of the Ascension
Emmanuel College Chapel, Cambridge
Acts 1.6–12

Dr Simone Kotva

In one of his gnomic poems, *Cherubic Wanderer III*, the seventeenth-century German mystic Angelus Silesius described the incarnation in the following words: 'Heaven humbles herself, towards earth makes its descent.' Heaven humbled herself by emptying herself, like a mother empties her womb; emptying herself of Christ, who walked among us. But this is only half the poem, which is concluded in the poignant question of the second line: 'When will the earth arise and become heaven-bent?'

At the Ascension, Christ unveils for us the answer to the poet's query. It is in the sudden retrieval of Christ from the midst of the apostles to the matrix of heaven that 'earth arises and becomes heaven-bent'.

Yet this upward ascent offers a strange, even a disquieting answer, since it robs us of our guide – mid-sentence, mid-teaching. It gives us no definitive solution to the 'when' of Silesius's question. Rather, the Ascension appears as a vanishing act, a particularly dramatic and bewildering underscoring to Christ's reprimand: 'It is not for you to know the times or periods that the Father has set by his own authority.'

This in reply to the apostles, who had asked, still clinging to the dream of a politically efficacious Messiah: 'Lord, is this the time when you will restore the kingdom to Israel?' But was theirs an unreasonable query? Or was it the desperate yearning of those who would prefer the events of Good Friday to have been a nightmare from which the risen Lord might awaken them? 'This time,' we hear them say, 'this once, surely our Lord will not fail us.' Not only for this reason do the apostles deserve our sympathy, but for the political nature of their question also. Their plea concerns 're-establishment', the concept that in Greek thought was known as *apokatastasis*. *Apokatastasis* was the time when all things in the world would 'stand up again' in their rightful place; when, according to some schools of Hellenistic philosophy, the world would be re-created anew out of the ashes of a cosmic conflagration. For the apostles, *apokatastasis* signifies not a general time, but a specific time of salvation, of worldwide political salvation: it is an end-time, the dawn of a new era. It is the hope for the future. If this is so, why are we offered this brusque pedagogy? Does not Christ encourage us continually to ready ourselves for the Kingdom of God; does not Revelation speak of a new earth, of a manner of *apokatastasis*?

For an answer, we must look to the repeated allusions to time that we find in our passage. The apostles are making a claim: the claim to be able to discern time, to know that 'this is the moment'; the time for action, the time for revolution. Thus the apostles are reprimanded: such knowledge belongs only to the creator of time, to God. But Christ voices his correction for a practical as well as metaphysical reason. To conceive of time as something that can be determined beforehand – that can be discerned – invites a certain complacent fatalism.

When the apostles, and we ourselves, speculate about time, the 'times or periods' (the *chronoi* and the *kairoi* in the Greek), these 'opportune moments' become something we wait for passively, rather than prepare for actively: rather than, that is, engage in the mission of discipleship, through which we prepare ourselves for God's time, whenever it may occur. This active preparation is needful because the unforeseen circumstances of Christ's incarnation – the humble manhood, the humbling even to death – has shown us that salvation is not reducible to a temporal 'moment' of measurable clock-time, to a dramatic coup d'état. The

Gospels show us how 're-establishment', *apokatastasis*, happened not on the battle field, but on the cross, and it happened in such a way that all of history, all of time, was transformed along with it, since it was performed by a man who was also God, who enfolds all of human time within the wondrous hyper-temporality that is Divine presence.

Together with the apostles, we are being charged with a more demanding mission than waiting for the 'right moment', a mission that will force us out of our reveries and millenarian calculations. It is the mission, as Christ tells us, to be witnesses not 'to the end of time' – for we are not, after all, immortal – but 'to the end of the earth', to its *eschatos*, its uttermost limit. To be witnesses, in other words, to the same earth whose realms we were set to work and tend at creation.

When Jesus suddenly is 'taken up', the 'two men in white', instil this lesson further. We read of how the apostles gaze as Christ is taken up, but when he disappears from their sight, they continue to gaze, and their gaze – which is our gaze – quickly becomes a gaze of nostalgia, of passive yearning. We wonder, desperately, if we shall ever see him again? The answer given by the dazzling messengers is again directed at our obsession with 'discerning the time', of scheduling our reunion with Christ: 'Why do you stand looking up toward heaven? This Jesus, who has been taken up from you into heaven, will come in the same way as you saw him go into heaven.'

Is it not enough to know that he will come again, and that we know how to recognize him when he does? With the knowledge of how in place of when, ours must be an active waiting, concerned not with the end of time but the geographical ends of earth: with the expanses and vast regions that encompass peoples, nations, politics and life, an earth that cannot be altered in a day, whose tending demands the service and sacrifice of all our individual lives.

Has this answered Silesius's question? Or do we find ourselves in a tragic suspense? Today it is two thousand years since the Ascension, and, as the secular critic would point out, it would seem that, ironically, Christ left at the right moment indeed. Did he not make an opportune escape, leaving the world to labour with the promise of a 'hope' that, every day, every year and every century grows weaker as the 'ends of the earth' are exploited and pockmarked by warfare?

But is the Ascension an abdication, truly a vanishing act? If we read closely, the passage suggests a different narrative.

Christ humbled himself, and left his Father's house to enter our own habitations, though our doors were not always open to him. Now Christ rises homeward: ascent is homecoming, the return to the hearth. In the Greek of our passage this moment is the *analepsis*, literally the 'taking back', the name by which the Feast of the Ascension is known in the Greek Orthodox Church. In Greek rhetoric, *analepsis* means an iteration, or an echoing of something that has gone before, particularly an iteration that 'brings home' the meaning to a narrative, bringing to it sense and conclusion.

The Ascension concludes in this way: the 40 days spent with the apostles repeat the 40 days spent in the wilderness, tempted by Satan; the ascent to heaven repeats the descent from heaven to earth in the incarnation, and continues and completes the ascent from hell to earth in the resurrection. And so, in later Greek, the *analeptikon*, the noun describing the thing that is 'taken back', is also a word describing the restorative drug, the medicine which re-establishes through repeating, through concluding, through coming home.

The Ascension is Christ as the restorative drug. With it he inaugurates the earth's bending towards heaven, but does not do so in order that the earth – with its suffering and violence – might be easily cast aside for the dream of an immediate, political 're-establishment'. The restorative drug is slow-working (unlike the deadly poison, which is instantaneous). And it is through protracted work, in spheres both public and private, that the Ascension itself can be concluded and continued; that heaven, like a lover, might bend towards earth, and earth, in reciprocity, might incline towards heaven. Through this labour we might establish the Kingdom of God in the ends of the earth.

This means also that Christ is a remedy that can never be said to have 'run its course'. His is an open conclusion, with a potency that is infinite, but whose efficacy demands the patient's consent. If we do not ingest, there will be no restoration. For with this medication was begun a transformation, which it is our calling, our terrifying but exhilarating imperative, to answer and to participate in, to our limits as we experience them both in this world, and in the hope of the one to come: both physical and spiritual. To this calling we were created to respond, but against this calling our political rhetoric of escapism – be it anarchic or conservative – now so vehemently rebels.

That is, we were created to be not like those soothsayers of the ancient world, the experts who attempted to descry the future – to discern the time – in the entrails of birds and the alignment of stars. I believe we were created to be more akin to the living birds themselves, the swallows who labour in joy, who live without the mediation of clocks and calculations; who soar, surge and swoop, yet in their quotidian ascension – minute, forgettable, unchronicled – bend and brush their wings against the very vault of heaven.

Love's Labour

Feast of St Philip and St James
Christ Church Cathedral, Oxford
John 14.1–14; 21.15–17

THE REVD CANON PROFESSOR GRAHAM WARD

On this eve when we celebrate the calling and discipleship of St Philip and St James, I want to look at what it means to be a disciple, a follower: indeed, a Christian. 'I am the way, the truth and the life,' Jesus tells us. But to understand this statement we need to look not at the passage from John's Gospel that we had read but a passage that comes at the end of that Gospel when the task of discipleship is made plain. That is, the famous dialogue between the risen Christ and Peter. And what we find is the central issue about following is: 'Do you love me?' This is what the risen Jesus asks Peter three times: 'Do you love me more than these?' This is the most basic question that Christ can ask of any who follow him; it's the basic ecclesiological question of belonging to Christ, of being *in* Christ. But as Peter recognizes, the one who asks this is the one who knows all things, God. Christ is therefore not asking Peter this question because he doesn't know the answer. He is asking it because Peter needs to know something – something about his own disposition now towards Christ; something that has changed because of the Easter events. Peter needs to know that he loves – and maybe that his loving, though beginning and ending in friendship, has to become self-sacrificial. Secondly, that loving carries consequences: feed or nourish my lambs, tend, guide, govern my sheep, feed or nourish my sheep.

To love in Christ installs us in sets of complex and dynamic relations that show us how Christ is the way, the truth and the life. Relations to ourselves; relations to Christ; relations to others. In this nexus of a dynamic set of relations, Peter himself will be hollowed out by that loving; that's what loving does. BUT, and this is crucial: being hollowed out in Christ is the most positive experience of redemption.

What Philip and James, and all of us, are called to is to love as a labour: a craft we have to learn, a craft in which we too have our being crafted. And this work cannot be done in our own strength. 'I have the power to lay down my life,' Jesus tells his gathered disciples, Philip and James among them. We don't have that power. If loving is done in our own strength, then the hollowing out that love produces can be dangerously negative and have profoundly damaging effects. The power of love comes from elsewhere, beyond us. It comes from God; it is God. It is a divine outpouring, *energeia*, out of which all things were created, in which we ourselves have our being. We are here because of love; love is written into our nature and our destiny. In all our loving of other people we are living out something of that divine love, we are exploring and experiencing that which is divine. In all our loving, we come to participate in Christ as the way, the truth and the life.

We are seeking; and no other person can fully satisfy what it is we are seeking for. Because the love we seek, in being divine, searches out the divine. It searches for what is eternal and uncreated. In all our human loving we are aspiring to know Christ, in whose image we were created, in whom and through whom all things were created, that we might attain that state spoken of by St Paul at the end of his paean to love in 1 Corinthians 13: to know even as we are known. No other person, in being loved and in loving us, can give us what we are demanding. With other human beings, living love on a purely human level, we either lose out, or come to a stable mutuality that protects us from that hollowing out that will always come as love does its work. When we know and understand the place of Christ in that love for another person then we will also recognize that we are each gifts to the other that we might learn Christ more deeply, be crafted by Christ more profoundly, and practise that feeding of the lambs and that tending of the sheep.

Love transforms. Its beginning and its end is a laying down of one's life, and that is so dangerous, and understood to be so dangerous, that many don't go there. They remain sealed up in themselves; or, rather, try to remain sealed up in themselves – because *amor sui* (love of self) is just as dangerous. *Amor sui* eats away at us, because it runs against everything written into our creation and all creation. Love has to be given. It has to be passed on. It has to be communicated – because it is God's communication to us, written into all things. It has to be practised in nurturing and feeding and tending and governing. That is love's *telos*. It is not a laying down for its own sake; and obedience has to proceed through discernment of the right time. Christ's crucifixion shows us that. It is not a laying down to get anything in return. It is a laying down in order to fulfil that which is love's destiny. BUT, and here's the paradox: the hollowing out that love performs is also a perfecting and fulfilling. In Greek: there can be no *kenosis* (self-emptying) without the *pleroma* (divine fullness). Love can only be lived in and through God.

We will fail; other people will always fail us – because what is demanded is too much, everything, and we are finite, creaturely. We will fail; other people will always fail us – because we are sinful. Love is the untying of all the knots of sinfulness. The knots that have been tied within us over generations and through those generations; the knots of self-interest and the knots of fear and shame and self-protection, all have to be untied. We have to be loosed from the selves that bind and limit us far beyond our finitude and creatureliness. But there will be no ministry, we will not be able to minister, or, rather, the people we minister to will only replicate the levels of tentative and frail freedom that have been crafted within us, unless we allow God's love to do its own divine work, its perfect work that brings us into perfection. That is redemption – and it is lived out. That is forgiveness – and it is lived out. That is the work of mercy over a lifetime of surrendered worship, discipleship and prayer.

The Language of Joy

Pentecost
Merton College Chapel, Oxford
Acts 2.1–21

THE RIGHT REVD DR JOHN INGE

And at this sound the crowd gathered and was bewildered, because each one heard them speaking in the native language of each (Acts 2.6).

As a youngster one of my party pieces was to recite the only Russian that my mother had taught me. I can still do it: *Ya gaviaroo parooski.* I thought it sounded rather impressive. I later learnt when visiting Russia that it is a singularly useless thing to say if it's the only Russian sentence you know. It means, as connoisseurs of the Russian language will be aware, 'I speak Russian'. I don't. Neither did my mother, capable though she was. *Ya gaviaroo parooski* was, for some obscure reason unknown to me, the only Russian sentence she had learnt. And she passed it on to me as part of a well-rounded education.

Language, after Babel, has been such a slippery thing. Translation can cause terrible misunderstandings: my mother had a French pen-friend as a child – you'll have gathered by now that she was a pretty cosmopolitan kind of woman – and this pen friend looked up the English equivalent for *Dieu vous préserve.* She then carefully inscribed at the end of her letter, 'God pickle you'.

The Holy Spirit, we infer from the reading from Acts we heard this evening, gives a common language that restores the confusion of Babel, for it will be understood by all. What is the language that we can expect to speak if we are filled with the Holy Spirit? I would like to suggest to you that it might be joy. Joy is, of course, one of the fruits of the Spirit. We learn in Acts 15.22 that the disciples were filled with joy and the Holy Spirit. Paul tells the Romans that the Kingdom of heaven is righteousness and peace and joy in the Holy Spirit and prays that they may be filled with all joy and hope in believing.

Christ came to bring joy: he speaks to his disciples of God's great love for them so that their joy may be complete. It permeates all that he says and does from the beginning of his ministry. As Dostoevsky writes in Chapter 4 of *The Brothers Karamazov*: 'Ah yes. I was missing that, and I don't want to miss it. I love that passage: it's Cana of Galilee, the first miracle. Ah that miracle! It was not men's grief but their joy Christ visited. He worked His first miracle to help men's gladness.'

I remember being very struck by a testimony that was given at a confirmation by a young woman whose heart was quite clearly bubbling over with joy. She recounted how her colleagues at work couldn't quite work out what was wrong with her. Conversely, Paul asks the Galatians, what has happened to all your joy? Doesn't this imply that lack of joy suggests a waning in Christian conviction? That great spiritual guide, Baron von Hügel, suggested that Newman had not been made a saint because he did not exhibit enough joy. I don't know whether that's true – and I'm not conversant with the method Roman Catholics use for determining who is a saint – but I do know that the Christians who have impressed me most are those who have clearly been filled with a deep-down joy.

One of the things that struck me about the young woman giving the testimony was that she couldn't stop laughing. Those who experienced the Toronto blessing were filled with laughter – and were treated with great suspicion as a result. Of course, the sort of joy to which the Scriptures are referring has nothing to do with a forced grin or inappropriate laughter. I do think, however, that laughter has more of a place in God's way with the world than is sometimes recognized and it's certainly *one* of the signs of joy. A facility to laugh often implies a godly perspective. To laugh is to rise above things so that we can see them in their true perspective, get them in proportion.

Sometimes we shall be weighed down by burdens and by evil – let's not underestimate its power. But it must not sully our joy because, as Paul emphasizes to the Romans, 'neither death, nor life, nor angels, nor rulers, nor things present, nor things to come, nor height, nor depth, nor anything else in all creation, will be able to separate us from the love of God in Christ Jesus our Lord' (Rom 8.38). That knowledge should carry us through the darkest of times in life. Archbishop Desmond Tutu has always struck me as someone full of joy and laughter. Surely this is a sign that he has been able to keep a godly perspective on things rather than be weighed down with the terrible situations that he has had to confront.

It might be thought that joy is different in character from the other gifts of the Spirit. There's something more active implied by love, peace, patience, kindness, generosity, faithfulness, gentleness and self-control, whereas joy is a state of being. If we can allow the Spirit to fill us with deep-down joy as we concentrate all our energy on the things of God, it will be infectious and we will be effective witnesses to the gospel. There was some research done by academics in Germany recently to investigate whether all the churches in the world that are growing, greatly different though they are, have anything in common. The answer, they found, was that they all exhibited joy and laughter in their common life.

People understand the language of joy, and they find it overwhelmingly attractive. I pray that the Holy Spirit will bring you joy, now and at all times, that it may be the language you speak. I pray that your hearts and minds may rise high with joy as did the hearts of the first disciples, as you remain close to the Lord in his word and sacrament, and in prayer. I pray that you may be given grace to rise above all the problems with which you have to cope as the Holy Spirit enables you to see them in a godly perspective – in the manner spoken of in a prayer from Michel Quoist's *Prayers of Life*, with which I conclude:

I would like to rise very high, Lord,
Above my city

Above the world

Above time,

I would like to purify my glance and borrow your eyes.

I would then see the universe, humanity, history as the
Father sees them.

I would see in the prodigious transformation of
matter, in the perpetual seething of life,

Your great body that is born of the breath of the Spirit.

I would see the beautiful, the eternal thought of your
Father's love taking form step by step,

Everything summed up in you, things on earth and things
in heaven.

And I would see that today like yesterday, the most
minute details are part of it ...

I would see the tiniest particle of matter and the smallest
throbbing of life,

Love and hate,

Sin and grace.

Startled, I would understand that the great adventure of
love, which started before the beginning of the world, is
unfolding before me,

The divine story which, according to your promise, will
be

completed only in glory after the resurrection of the flesh,

When you come before the Father, saying, All is
accomplished, I am Alpha and Omega, the beginning and
end ...

Then, falling on my knees, I would admire, Lord, the
mystery of this world

Which, in spite of the innumerable and hateful snags.
  of sin,
Is a long throb of love, towards love eternal.[19]

Finding Ourselves in the Trinity

Trinity Sunday
Keble College, Oxford
Isaiah 6.1–8; Romans 8.12–17; John 3.1–17

THE REVD DR ALISON MILBANK

On the feast of the Trinity let us pray to the Holy and Undivided Trinity, in John Keble's own words, that God might 'help us each hour, with steadier eye/ To search the deepening mystery'. Amen.

It is a great pleasure to be with you at the culmination of the liturgical cycle of the birth, life and death of Christ: at the celebration of the descent of the Holy Spirit on Christ's disciples. Now this all becomes our own story, and we take time today to think, as the early Church began to do, about what it all means: what does the drama of the life of Jesus tell us about the nature of God himself?

For the doctrine of the Trinity is not an academic game: it is our faith. In that doctrine we live and move and have our being. It matters. Orthodoxy does not just mean 'right belief' but right honour or praise; and the Trinity shapes and orders our life as a community caught up in worship into the deepening divine mystery in company with the angels and archangels. I want to suggest to you that in learning about the Trinitarian life of God we also learn about ourselves. For in worship, in relation to God, we are our most real: we find our true selves in God.

Our three readings help us to understand this and share an

emphasis on the human person's response. First, the great prophet Isaiah has a vision of the glory of God filling the Temple: what is called a theophany. The choir will sing the words of the seraphim in Isaiah's vision during the eucharistic prayer in the Sanctus: 'Holy, holy, holy, Lord God of Hosts', for then we shall indeed be taken into heaven. Isaiah is overcome by the divine otherness, the blazing purity and unity of God – and he is terrified at his own incapacity to survive that dangerous holiness. Help, however, comes from God in the purifying coal and Isaiah is able to find words to respond: 'Here am I; send me!' Paradoxically, the otherness, the transcendence of God, calls the human being into relation. The triple repetition of 'holy' in this heavenly song is a Hebrew mode of emphasis, but Christians found in it a deeper significance, that the unity of God has something threefold about it, and similarly our own participation in him.

St Paul explores the way we share in God's threefold life in our passage from the letter to the Romans. Again it is through worship: 'When we cry, "Abba! Father!" it is the very Spirit bearing witness with our spirit that we are children of God.' How can we do this? It was not usual to address God as 'father' in Judaism; it was Jesus who taught his followers to do that, in the Lord's Prayer. We know God as Father through Christ as his son: the persons of the Trinity are a series of relations. Here through Christ we are caught up into the mystery of that relation between Father and Son. We can be part of that abiding in love which they share, through the gift of the Holy Spirit, which speaks with us, as it were, witnessing to our adoption and incorporation in one and the same action as he reveals God as Father. Augustine, at the end of the fourth century, developed this idea of the Spirit as the witness, and used it to argue that the Spirit was the witness of the love of the Father for the Son, and Son for Father because he *is* that bond of love: in his own person he reveals that love. Our true destiny, as adoptive children, is to be witnesses of it also – just as adoptive children in loving families do know the embrace of a love that is overwhelming, moving beyond the tie of blood kinship.

Our Gospel reading develops this meditation on how we share

the Trinitarian life. 'You must be born from above', Christ tells the enquirer, Nicodemus. Not only does the Son descend from heaven but we must be taken up. We tend to think of baptism as a going down, and so it is. We descend into the waters of death to be reborn, but that rebirth is a heavenly one. This passage from John is full of movements up and down: in Christ, who was lifted up on a cross to die, we see God. The way up is the way down and the way down is the way up. No wonder Nicodemus is confused! In relation to the mystery of the incarnation and the nature of God we all, like Nicodemus, 'come by night'. We enter a paradoxical mystery in which we seek to hold together the God who is utterly holy and beyond our comprehension and a God who 'came down' to show himself in his Son. He sent his Spirit, furthermore, to dwell in our own bodies, so that God is nearer to us than the eyelashes lying on our cheek.

Human beings need a God who is wholly beyond us to recognize that we are creatures, and to see in our own unknowable depths the divine. Our lives are so disordered and fractured by constant demands, the glamour of objects of desire, multiplicity of operations, that we have no unity in our own self. Isaiah's 'Woe is me, I am lost' is our own cry – we are lost in a thousand instagrams or takeaway cappuccinos. We are so rarely present to ourselves, able to be in the moment: to really live. We need God to call us into relation, and to collect us. For in that birthing by the Spirit from on high we are able to name that otherness as Father and know him through the Son.

For it is only through faith in Christ as Son and image of the Father that we can become God's children, and come to love ourselves as the Father loves us. Jesus uses the analogy of the brazen serpent that Moses put on a pole. When the Israelites, suffering from snake-bite, looked at it, they were healed. Christ as the image of the Father is the agent of our own healing, 'to the end that all that believe in him should not perish but have everlasting life' (John 3.16). We look at Christ on the cross and see the love of the Father for and through the Son, and that love comes to birth in us – and saves us.

The next time that you dig out an old diary, essay or poem

you have written and think, 'Did I really write that?', surprising yourself with an understanding or ability you did not realize you had, that is a sign in you of your own mystery, that you are not, in fact, your own, but live in relation to the ultimate depth of reality that is God. Your act of realization is the work of Christ, the Son, who is God's self-understanding in which he knows you and you know yourself. And God loves you through his Spirit, by which you love and are drawn to love others, so that you too can say 'Here am I, send me'. This language sounds close to the modern cult of 'finding yourself' but is so different. It is not my little buffered, atomized autonomous subjectivity that is real, but God. As Dante writes in the final canto of *Paradise*: God is 'Light eternal, who alone abides in yourself, alone knows yourself, and, known to yourself and knowing, loves and smiles on yourself'. We become real in God and only in God do we find ourselves. So may the Trinity draw us ever further into the divine activity, knowing and loving, and may we too be sent to draw others into that ecstatic, eternal dance.

V

For the Time Being:
Trinity Season and Christian Lives

Ordinary or ordered time turns attention to the Christian living out of the life of Christ, once the cycle of mimetic imitation of his earthly life opens out to the Feast of Corpus Christi and beyond. As a day of 'Thanksgiving for Holy Communion', Corpus Christi has again been owned by the Anglican Church, but its particular richness comes from the idea of ourselves as taken up with the elements into the transformative act of God in the sacrament, so that we as a body become the body of Christ. The communal nature of our life in Christ is central to this feast and to the saints' days, which adorn this time, leading up to All Saints. In our introduction, we were unrepentant about the sometimes legendary developments of the lives of holy men and women, because such lives are generative of faith and further story. We still need St George to point out the dragons of want and greed, and tell us to fight them in society and in our own souls. The holy angels remind us that we are not God's only creation, and that the world is charged with his love and knowledge, mediated to us through hidden powers.

Ecological concerns, as well as the rise of neo-paganism, have also drawn the Church back to the cycle of the agricultural year, upon which we all depend, and in which preaching can help to bring out the theological richness of Lammas and Harvest, and the challenge to our greed and injustice.

Our final section offers examples of sermons to accompany occasional offices and rites of passage. They reveal how the personal opens to the ecclesial, and how a life, lay or clerical, becomes exemplary and generative. This whole section is inflected by the theology of gift, which is a central feature of radically orthodox thought. In contrast to much gift theory, we stress not only the originating gift of God but its call for response and being taken up as gift and giver in acts of reciprocal exchange.

Preaching itself is never an originating act by the one speaking, but a response to the divine Spirit whose gifts make possible our speech. It aims to empower the people of God to respond to the Word heard in our words, and to be formed by the Spirit into active receivers, who themselves will share those gifts with others. Thomas Aquinas believed that we are made in the image of God as the one who gives life and freedom, so that we too may give life and freedom to that which we make. May our words too share that generative generosity, to fly from us, to be shaped and remade in the thoughts and actions of others.

Consume and Be Consumed

Feast of Corpus Christi
St Michael's Church, Abingdon
John 6.47–52

The Revd Dr Gregory Platten

Last December saw the World Mince Pie Eating Competition, held at Wookey Hole in Somerset. The winner was a surprisingly diminutive young girl – Sonya Thomas – who consumed a record 46 mince pies in under ten minutes. I later worked out that's an incredible 11,500 calories in ten minutes. If you are interested, that is six days' worth of energy for the average female, all eaten in under ten minutes.

Calories are, of course, the scientific measurement of energy. At this Eucharist tonight, though, here in Abingdon, we are to eat food that, superficially, contains only a tiny few calories, and yet it has within it the raw energy of God. This bread and wine is indeed the very leaven of immortality. Thanksgiving for Holy Communion, therefore, is not thanking God for the gift of a service, weekly or daily enjoyed. It is, rather, thanksgiving for God's gift of himself in his enfleshed Son; thanksgiving for his incarnation, for Jesus, through whom he has led us to share in the divine world.

The Feast of Corpus Christi emerged in the mediaeval period. Of course, the other great day when we remember the eucharistic foundations of our faith is Maundy Thursday. We recall the final supper of Christ with his friends in an upper room, hidden away from the anger of resentful doubters. Yet it is not possible to celebrate with true elation and ecstasy when the following day we remember the goring passion of our Lord on Good Friday. It was a rather persistent nun, one Juliana of Liège, who received mystical visions in which God had suggested that there ought to be a feast day for the Eucharist. After lengthy petitioning, she persuaded an influential local Dominican, the Archdeacon of Liège and the Bishop to introduce a grand local feast purely for the 'Mass' (such was the independence of bishops in those days in the Church of Rome) in 1246. Later on, following claims of a miracle involving a consecrated chalice of Christ's blood, the same local archdeacon (one Jacques Pantalaéon) who, now made Pope Urban IV, finally decided that Corpus Christi, the body of Christ, should be a feast celebrated throughout the Church. That was in 1264.

We may not call it Corpus Christi in Anglican speak, just as we prefer Communion or Eucharist to Mass, some even drearily limiting it to the 'Lord's Supper', which makes it sound like a special at the local Harvester. And yet, despite our Anglican reserve, it is quite right and proper that Anglicans celebrate our Lord's great and simple command uttered in the upper room, 'do this in remembrance of me'; those words are still followed in most churches and in most lands throughout the world.

This is mysterious and mystical, for this is not simply a set of words and actions; this is a feast that brings us into God's nearer presence, to be participants in the divine life. Let us never forget how scandalous and extraordinary the gospel words of Christ must have sounded to the ears of those who first heard, when he calls himself the 'bread of life':

Very truly, I tell you, whoever believes has eternal life. I am the bread of life. Your ancestors ate the manna in the wilderness, and they died. This is the bread that comes down from heaven, so that one may eat of it and not die. I am the living bread that came down from heaven. Whoever eats of this bread will live forever; and the bread that I will give for the life of the world is my flesh. (John 6.47–51)

There is no currency in the words of those who seek to soften this message, for it is stark and unnerving, the sundering of the divisions between earth and heaven. There is the physical and there is the spiritual; the boundaries between each are firmly drawn. That is, until Christ. Suddenly, what is divine, above and beyond, breaks in. Suddenly that which is intangible and 'of the soul' has cut through the thin veil and become physical *incarne*, there in meat, in flesh. In Christ, there is no nature and supernature; all is one cosmos, one whole. It is his flesh that he offers for our food and for our salvation. That is at the heart of the Eucharist and Communion. As the hymn goes: 'types and shadows have their ending; for the newer rite is here'.

We *eat Christ*, we actually *eat him*, and take him into ourselves. But it is not cannibalism. Cannibalism is eating another fellow human; to eat Christ is to take God into ourselves. And here is when we need to worship with awe the mystery at the heart of the Eucharist. Christ promises us, as he did to Paul and his other earliest followers, that in bread broken and shared, in wine blessed and drunk from the cup, he is here with us. God transforms himself, through his Son, so that he can be as one with us, bone of our bone, flesh of our flesh, as close to us as the blood in our veins.

Lives have been lost, churches torn apart trying to define this great and tremendous mystery, hours spent trying to describe the technical details. Some have bought into the Aristotelian terms of transubstantiation, while others preferred the reformed memorialism of Zwingli. These extremes have rather missed the point. That bread becomes body and wine becomes blood is no problem to be solved, rather it is a mystery to be adored and praised. For it is this extraordinary transformation that means we take into ourselves, into our bodies, the body of Christ. Christ is physically incorporated within us; and through his dwelling within us, we are sanctified, drawn up inescapably into the divine. And as each is united with Christ, we are all united as one. This is communion by consumption. St John Chrysostom, in a homily on this same gospel passage, wrote:

143

We become one Body, and 'members of His flesh and His bones'. (Eph. 5.30). Let the initiated follow what I say. In order then that we may become this not by love only, but in very deed, let us be blended into that flesh ... He hath mixed up Himself with us; He hath kneaded up His body with ours, that we might be a certain One Thing, like a body joined to a head.[20]

We give thanks for the Eucharist, because the Eucharist is itself the giving thanks. In this service, word and action unite the divided parties of the world kneeling at one rail, bonded by one bread and body. At the same time earth and heaven unite too, witnessing the thin veil lifted. In this service, we are gathered up into the incarnation and redemption of Christ. This is no re-enactment, nor replay. This is none other than a foretaste of the heavenly banquet and we are fed with resurrection food.

Call it Mass, call it Communion, call it the Eucharist if you will. For me, they will always be known as the Holy Mysteries. For what can be more mysterious than the fact that the one we consume each time we meet together to give thanks is the very one that consumes us utterly, enfolding us in love, and giving us abundant life beyond decay and death. This truly is a fascinating and awesome mystery.

The Sound of Silence

First Sunday of Trinity
Church of the Holy Family, Chapel Hill, North Carolina
1 Kings 19.1–15; Psalms 42 and 43; Galatians 3.23–29; Luke
8. 26–39

STANLEY HAUERWAS

There is no longer Jew or Greek, there is no longer slave or free, there is no longer male and female; for all of you are one in Christ Jesus. And if you belong to Christ, then you are Abraham's offspring, heirs according to the promise (Gal. 3.28–29).

'Finally,' like me, you have to be thinking, 'finally'! Finally we have a Paul that does not embarrass us. We have had to struggle with Paul's seeming indifference to slavery; we have cringed at some of his judgements about the place of women in the Church; we have had to put up with his judgemental attitude about sex; but now it seems we have a Paul with whom we share some fundamental convictions.

After all, what could be more precious to us than the democratic commitment to treat all people equally? We want everyone to be treated fairly. We want to be treated fairly. Not only at work and home, but also in church. The Church accordingly should be inclusive, excluding no one. In this passage from Galatians Paul seems to be on the side of equal treatment. He finally got one right.

There is just one problem with our attempt to read Paul as an advocate of democratic egalitarianism. As much as we would like

145

to think that Paul is finally on the right side of history, I am afraid that reading this text as an underwriting of egalitarian practice is not going to work. Paul does not say Jew or Greek, slave or free, male or female are to be treated equally. Rather he says that all who make up the Church in Galatia, and it is the Church to which he refers, are one in Christ Jesus. It seems that Jew and Greek, slave and free, male and female have been given a new identity more fundamental than whether they are a Jew, slave or free. In so far as they now are in the Church they are all one in Christ.

For Paul our unity in Christ seems to trump equality. Let me suggest that this is not necessarily bad news for us, because one of the problems with strong egalitarianism is how it can wash out difference. In truth, most of us do not want to be treated like everyone else because we are not simply anyone. Whatever defeats and victories have constituted our lives they are our defeats and victories and they make us who we are. We do not want to be treated equally if that means the history that has made us who we are must be ignored. For example, I think being a Texan is one of the determinative ontological categories of existence. I would never say I just happen to be a Texan because being a Texan, particularly in North Carolina, is a difference I am not about to give up in the hope of being treated fairly.

But what does it mean to be 'one in Christ Jesus'? Some seem to think being one in Christ means Christians must be in agreement about matters that matter, and especially about the beliefs that make us Christian. The problem with that understanding is that there has been no time in the history of the Church when Christians have been in agreement about what makes us Christians. To be sure, hard-won consensus has from time to time been achieved, but usually the consensus sets the boundaries for the ongoing arguments we need in order to discern what we do not believe.

This disagreement is not necessarily the result of some Christians holding mistaken beliefs about the faith. We are a people scattered around the world who discover different ways of being Christian, given the challenges of particular contexts and times in which we find ourselves. If we were poor we might, for example, better understand the role of Mary in the piety of many that identify themselves as Roman Catholics.

If unity was a matter of agreement about all matters that matter, it clearly would be a condition that cannot be met. We certainly cannot meet the demand here at Holy Family. For example, I happen to know some of you are fans of the New York Yankees. Clearly we have deep disagreements that will not be easily resolved. So it surely cannot be the case our unity in Christ Jesus is a unity that depends on our being in agreement about all matters that matter.

There is another way to construe what it might mean to be one in Christ Jesus that I think is as problematic as the idea that our unity should be determined by our being a people who share common judgements about what makes us Christian. Some, for example, seem to think that unity is to be found in our regard for one another. We are united because we are a people who care about one another. Some even use the language of love to characterize what it means for us to be united in Christ.

The problem with that way of construing our unity is it is plainly false. We do not know one another well enough to know if we like, much less love, one another. Of course it is true that you do not have to like someone to love them, but I suspect that, like me, you tend to distrust anyone who claims to love you but does not know you. If love, as Iris Murdoch suggests, is the nonviolent apprehension of the other as other, then you cannot love everyone in general. The love that matters is that which does not fear difference. Christians are, of course, obligated to love one another and such love may certainly have a role to play in our being one in Christ Jesus. But that does not seem to be what Paul means in this letter to the Galatians.

Paul seems to think that what it means for us to be one in Christ Jesus is a more determinative reality than our personal relations with one another make possible. Indeed when unity is construed in terms of our ability to put up with one another the results can be quite oppressive. For the demand that we must like or even love one another can turn out to be a formula for a church in which everyone quite literally is alike. A friendly church can be a church that fears difference. As much as we might regret it, I suspect it remains true that those we like, and perhaps even love, are those who are just like us. Whatever it means, therefore, for us to be one in Christ Jesus it surely cannot mean that we must like one another.

How then are we to understand what it means to be one in Christ Jesus? Paul says that if we belong to Christ we are Abraham's offspring and heirs according to God's promise that he would make us his people. Once we were no people but now we are a people who through baptism have been clothed anew by Christ. What it means for us to be one in Christ is to be a people who have been given a new story. We are the children of Abraham, which means that the kind of struggle against idolatry that Elijah faced is now part of our history. We are one with our Jewish brothers and sisters because together we face a world that knows not the God who refuses to let Elijah accept defeat.

The very fact that the Old Testament is Christian Scripture means the story of Israel's faithfulness, trials and persecutions must illumine our life as the Church of Jesus Christ. For example, I suspect there are few things we do as Christians more important than pray the psalms. The psalms give voice to Israel's faith in God even when the enemies of that faith, the Ahabs and Jezebels, seem to have the upper hand. Thus Israel asks,

> Why have you forgotten me?
> And why do I go so heavily while the enemy oppresses me?
> While my bones are being broken,
> my enemies mock me to my face;
> All day long they mock me
> and say to me, 'Where now is your God?' (Ps. 42.9–11)

'Where now is your God?' is a question that haunts us, not because we do not believe in God, but because we simply don't know how to answer it. We stammer for explanations. We believe God remains present in this world – in our lives. And we want desperately to believe we have been made one with Christ Jesus, but that seems like some ideal that has little bearing on reality. In fact, the evidence seems to testify to God's absence. To read the psalms is to discover that the current challenges posed by the 'new atheists' to the faith are not nearly as significant as those voiced by the Psalmist. Thus Elijah asks God to take his life because, being 'no better than his ancestors', he assumes his situation is hopeless. What can it mean for this to be the history that makes us one with Christ?

I think it has everything to do with learning to hear, as Elijah does, God's silence. Better put: it means that we become for the world God's silence so that the world may know that the salvation offered by God is not just another failed ideal. Elijah stands on the mountain to be encountered by God. There is a mighty wind, but the Lord is not in the wind, God is not in the earthquake, nor is God to be found in the fire. Rather God is in what is described as 'the sound of sheer silence', a silence we are told that Elijah heard. We cannot help but wonder how silence can have a sound that can be heard, but then we must remember that this is God who is passing by Elijah.

I suspect if you are like me you would prefer a God who chooses to be in the wind, earthquake or fire. We want a God who leaves little doubt about what it means to be God. We are not at all sure we want to be a people capable of hearing the 'sound of silence'. To hear the sound of silence means we face a God we cannot make serve our peculiar purposes. Like Elijah we must first listen.

In truth, I find listening to be a hard discipline. I am seldom silent. I am, after all, an academic. I am not supposed to be at a loss for words. I am to be the kind of person who always has something to say. To learn first to be silent, to listen, threatens loss of control. My only power is the power of the word. So I try to anticipate what you are going to say prior to your saying it so that I can respond before you have said anything.

I try to play the same game with God. I want God to be loquacious. I want God to be like me. But God is not like me. That God is present in silence suggests that listening to silence is as essential as listening to what God says. This is what Elijah had learned about the God of Israel. And this is what we must learn if we are to hear the word of the Lord today. For the same Word that speaks to us today has spoken through the prophets. And God has not left us without resources for learning to be faced by silence.

What it means for us to be one in Christ, moreover, I think we discover in the silence that engulfs as we confront the most decisive moment of God's silence, that is, the crucifixion. That is when we learn to listen to the sheer silence of our God. That is the moment we discover we are one in Christ Jesus. During Holy Week we hear again how our Lord is silent before his accusers. On Maundy Thursday we kneel in silence as the body and blood of our Saviour is carried away, the nave is stripped, and we leave the church. That silence, the stunning silence of the crucifixion, is the silence of our God who refuses to save us by violence. The silence of Jesus is echoed by the silence of those who helplessly stood by with his holy mother to bear witness to his silent submission to the Father's will, for our sake. It is this silence that makes us one with him in a manner more determinative than our agreements or commonalities.

This means that there are times when asked, 'Where now is your God?' we had best remain silent. Yet it is enough. By learning to be silent we have learned to be present to one another and the world as witnesses to the God who has made us a people who once were no people. Such a people have no need to pretend that we know more about our God than we do. We need not pretend that we do not face the reality of death and how that reality makes us doubt if our lives have purpose. But we believe we have been given every gift needed to remain faithful. Just as Elijah was commanded to eat so that he would have strength for the journey, so we have been given this bread and wine which, through the power of the Holy Spirit, makes us one with and in Christ Jesus.

'There is no longer Jew or Greek, there is no longer slave or free, there is no longer male and female; for all of you are one in Christ Jesus.' This is indeed good news, but the new identity we have in Christ is one that cannot be attested to by words. The words we use must be surrounded by the silence of God. To belong to Christ, to belong to one another, means we must, like Christ – and like Elijah before him – trust in the sound of that silence.

Witness to the Depths of God

Feast of St Mary Magdalene, Apostle
St Mary Magdalen's, Oxford
John 20.1–18

THE RIGHT REVD STEPHEN CONWAY

I am glad that your vicar here at St Mary Magdalen's does not hold with the association of your patron with the woman who bathes Jesus' feet with her tears. I myself am more drawn to the earlier traditions about Mary Magdalene as evangelist and contemplative than to the Renaissance fantastical emphasis on her as a courtesan. However, I love the daring of Caravaggio who chooses a courtesan to be his model both for Mary Magdalene and for the Blessed Virgin. It is wonderful to have provoked the Church to see them both as completely flesh-and-blood women. My profound belief, however, is that Mary Magdalene provokes us fully to see what it might mean for someone recovering from severe and enduring mental illness to be an apostolic witness for Jesus.

Our reading from St John's Gospel is set in a garden, and I wish to begin in a Cambridge garden. There is a shed in the garden of the Anglican theological college, Westcott House, which sports the sign 'Canon in Residence'. The gardener is a retired priest who served as a senior mental health chaplain and family therapist. His shed is for potting and consulting. I did a life-changing placement with this priest at a hospital for the mentally ill myself when I was an ordinand at Westcott House.

We instinctively shy away from people who are mad because it could so easily be us. These people can occasionally be dangerous but mostly they are harmless and desperately isolated in the howling wilderness of their illness. They are isolated further by the fact that mental illness still carries the stigma of moral failure that no longer applies to most physical illnesses. We have come to see how narrow the boundary is between genius and madness. We can all too fearfully see a continuum between our down-in-the-mouth days and serious depressive illness. Recognizing this fear in myself, I arranged to spend two weeks on an acute admissions ward of the local mental hospital, not as a member of staff but in the patient area. I encountered some very distressed and quite distressing people. I met our Lord God many times on the ward.

My last sentence was intended to be double-edged. I met people claiming to be God Almighty; but I also met Jesus in these people. Each morning there was an optional prayer meeting in the chaplain's office. One day he arranged to be absent so that I would have to preside. There were five or six of us, one of whom was a young woman who attended a charismatic church. She began to weep uncontrollably as soon as we started the Lord's Prayer. 'How can God do this to me? I have been born again. Why is he so far from me?'

I did not have the faintest idea what to do, but help was at hand. Another member of the group was Nora. She always had her hat and coat on, ready to go home, even though her home circumstances were precisely what drove her every few months back to the hospital. A cigarette was always poised precariously on her lower lip. I had never known her to say anything coherent or sensible. But just then she pointed a skeletal finger at a large crucifix on the wall and said: 'Look at him. He knows. He's one of us. He's the friend of Mary Magdalene. And take your medicine.' She then lapsed back into her mumbling.

I see much contemporary corroboration of the evidence from the Gospels that Jesus had a special relationship with people who were deemed mad. The crowds gathered primarily because of his reputation as an exorcist and healer. And it was the mad people, like Legion and others, who first knew who Jesus was. 'Son of God', they shouted, 'Have you come to torment us before the time?' (Matt. 8.29). But he brought not torment, but release and healing. Among these people, we are told that Jesus had healed Mary of Magdala, who had been released of seven devils.

At first sight, this seems like an inauspicious beginning for the apostle to the apostles. Here was someone who had been locked in another world, and yet she is clearly a trusted friend. Not so long ago, I confirmed a couple who both live with lasting mental ill-health. Andy, who was also blind, offered his testimony. He joked that, having been sectioned 28 times, he was glad that at last his religious delusions were being taken seriously. The next time I met him was at a service to commission a priest to work with the homeless and mentally ill. Andy spoke the Gospel reading without hesitation from memory. He spoke with authority about the transforming presence of Christ. My encounters with people who live with severe depression or psychotic illness have taught me that people who live metaphorically with fewer layers of skin than some can be eloquent witnesses to the depths of God, and to the power of the resurrection in dark places of crucifixion. Such people have been decisive witnesses in my life.

There is a strong tradition that Mary Magdalene escaped persecution in Palestine and came to Provence. Here she first had a ministry as an evangelist, sharing her experience of Jesus and her testimony to his resurrection. Like many apostolic saints after her, we are told that she spent her last years in reparation in a cave. When the Renaissance sculptor, Donatello, was in his seventies he carved some studies in age, among them a carving of an aged Mary Magdalene. She is depicted as an ascetic and hermit. She is haggard and it is impossible to know where her rags and wild hair overlap. Every spiritual battle is written there in the plain wood. The wonderful discovery, however, is that the careful restoration of the statue a few years ago revealed that Donatello had used the finest gold leaf to signify a life shot through with glory. This is us, too, as we begin to see more clearly the glory with which the world is shot through like strands of beautiful silk. Part of our brokenness is inhabited as we realize how blind to this glory much of world chooses to be.

Mary Magdalene discovered that she need no longer be defined as a person by the isolation of her illness aggravated by other people's opinions. She could accept the restoration of the inner beauty that is the birth-right of the sons and daughters of God. Accepting all that had happened to her, she took it all to Jesus and he blessed her. She was being made ready to follow Jesus in the Way.

Yet, when it came to the resurrection, Mary does not see it to begin with. For her, like Thomas, being told about the resurrection of Jesus was not enough. They have to sense it for themselves – in Mary hearing her name being called and in Thomas probing the wounds. Imagine Mary in her grief, moving into shock as she sees that the tomb is empty and that there are angels present telling her news that she just cannot compute. But then she hears his voice; the voice she did not recognize before; the voice she did not understand until it speaks her name, and then she is free of the grief and begins to feel the great joy that we are to feel this day – and indeed through our whole lives.

When Mary encounters the risen Christ in the garden, she does not recognize Jesus at first: in the resurrection that Jesus does not look the same. But the two things that are recognizable about Jesus in the garden are his voice and his wounds. We should do all in our power to be effective witnesses to the world of what Mary saw. However, there is no way round the truth that we have to sense the resurrection for ourselves. The living proof of the resurrection of Christ is my inner hearing of Jesus calling me by name and his transforming my identity as someone who then goes out looking for his new creation in the vitality and love and thirst for justice I see in other people. We may see what seem like small shoots in food banks and good neighbourliness; but all this is witness to the resurrection of Jesus even in crucifixion situations. Jesus told Mary not to cling to his new body because that was not going to be permanently available to the disciples she represents like you and me. He does not want her to have to grieve all over again. He will be present everywhere and forever in his Spirit and it is that Spirit who is leading us always to new life in the garden of God's delight.

If Jesus is recognizable by his scars, perhaps it is also true that we shall be very different in our resurrection bodies, too, but still recognizably ourselves in our scars. We can so easily live the resurrection intellectually and believe in our heads that it is all true, but somehow not believe in our hearts that all can be forgiven and all can ultimately be healed in our lives. Well, just think what it might be like to be recognizable by the sign of the healing of every single hurt we have ever known.

St Mary Magdalen's is a church that famously generates vocations to the priesthood among young women and men. On the surface, it looks like a very foolish thing to do – making sacrifices, giving up the prospect of a substantial income; but many from here have and do catch the vision of the divine foolishness which is worth giving one's life to. The foolishness that God desires of us all as his disciples and as followers of our patron and all the saints is like this. In Shakespeare's *King Lear*, the King's only constant friend is the Fool. It is he who speaks wisdom to the worldly monarch and at the last he is hanged for his devotion. Lear himself only finds redemption when he goes mad. Donatello's statue has Mary Magdalene on the front foot. All that she has been through and endured is not holding her back. She is still ready to respond to the voice of Jesus calling her by name. She knows that God may well call us to be broken, but never to be destroyed. He has called us by name and made us his own for ever.

The Beauty in the Ugliness

Feast of the Transfiguration
St Michael's, Exeter
1 John 3.1; Luke 9.28–36

THE REVD DR JOHN HUGHES

The appearance of his face changed, and his clothes became dazzling white. (Luke 9.29)

Was Jesus 'good-looking', was he handsome, or a 'babe' as the contemporary jargon might have it? Was the Saviour of the World a Clark Gable or a Johnny Depp of his day? This might seem like the sort of frivolous and irreverent question we might find in the popular press. And yet, it was a question that occupied some of the great Fathers of the early Church. For it was to them a serious theological problem: there are no accounts in the Gospels of what Christ looked like, but if, as they believed, he is the Son of God, perfect humanity taken up by the Word of God in the incarnation, then perhaps, they reasoned, his perfection should extend also to his appearance. In the first-century Mediterranean world, there were very clear canons of what the perfect man and woman should look like, and so some of the earliest representations of Christ take on these ideas of beauty, showing him either as the young hero after Apollo, or as the wise bearded philosopher-statesman after Alexander the Great. To support this view of Christ as perfect in beauty, the Fathers cited various passages from the Old Testament: 'You are the fairest of the sons of men; grace is poured upon your lips; therefore God has blessed you for ever' (Ps. 45.2).

But in addition to these Old Testament verses that spoke of the Messiah as radiant and beautiful, there were others that struck a contradictory note: 'his appearance was so marred, beyond human semblance, and his form beyond that of the sons of men' (Isa. 52.14). Perhaps this seems to us more in keeping with the historical reality: Jesus was not a model, a hero, but a Jewish peasant and one whose death particularly was one of the ugliest imaginable. So, which of these two ideas is correct? The beautiful Christ or the ugly Christ?

I think this problem is part of the festival we celebrate today: the Feast of the Transfiguration of Our Lord. 'Transfiguration' means to change shape or appearance. Fairy tales often involve some form of transfiguration, whether it's the frog who turns into a prince when kissed, or Cinderella whose pumpkin is transformed into a carriage to take her to the ball. The point of such changes of appearances is normally to show that 'things aren't always what they seem', how easily we can be tricked by appearances, and how there is a deeper seeing we need to learn, which can see the beautiful even in what at first appears ugly.

In our Gospel reading, Jesus takes his closest disciples apart and goes with them up a mountain, where they see him transfigured by divine light, that most ancient symbol of heavenly beauty, like the glory that accompanied the giving of the commandments on Mount Sinai, and joined by Moses and Elijah, representing the highest figures of the Jewish tradition which Christ fulfils. This is a funny event in the gospel narratives, because it is as if, for a brief moment, we get a peek at the end of the story, in the middle, rather like turning to the last page of a murder novel to find out whodunnit. Here, as the events of Christ's life move towards their ugly and awful dénouement, the disciples, who are pretty confused as to what's going on at this point, are granted a brief foretaste of what will come after the ugliness: the beauty and glory of the risen Christ on Easter morn. Here they see that in and through and beyond the ugly horrors of the cross, the suffering and self-sacrifice, comes the ever-greater return of God's beautiful love. The Transfiguration is the beginning of the disciples learning this difficult and paradoxical lesson, learning to see the beauty in the ugliness.

In answer to our original question, then, it seems both sides were right: Christ is both ugly *and* beautiful: ugly to worldly eyes in his total identification in love with the outcaste, the hated, the poor and suffering, even unto that ugliest of all things, death; and yet at the same time, beautiful in the infinite attraction of divine love, radiant with the life and glory of the Father.

But all this does not just apply to Christ. Because, just as the Transfiguration is a foretaste of the glory of Easter, so Easter is a foretaste of the glory that will be bestowed upon *all* of us in heaven. For then, as Christ says, elsewhere, 'the righteous will shine like the sun', radiant with the same glory and love that the disciples saw on the mount of the Transfiguration. Or as we heard in the Epistle today: 'when he shall appear we shall be like him'. Our true, beautiful selves are already 'hidden with Christ' in God, rather like Dorian Gray's portrait in the attic, except that painting showed his true ugliness rather than his true beauty. And our radiant beauty is not just confined to the future, to heaven, but is already breaking in here and now, as we begin to see the world through God's eyes. This is why saints are always painted with a halo of light, and even if this might not be immediately obvious, surely most of us have known those whose lives, when we see beyond the surface, shine with compassion and holy joy and simple goodness. They are truly radiant and beautiful, even if we don't see it immediately, and such people transfigure the world around them, lifting up the despised and unloved, turning their lives around, bringing hope out of despair and joy out of sorrow and anger.

In our culture, we are perhaps more trained than any other generation before *not* to see beyond the superficiality of the surface, the accents, the hair styles, the designer clothes. And yet God is continually at work, in a thousand small ways, for those who have eyes to see, transfiguring this world of sin and making it radiant with the beauty of divine love. Here today we are called to join in that work, to see the world being transfigured, to be transfigured ourselves, and to transfigure those around us, beginning now from this Eucharist, where the ordinary things of bread and wine are transfigured into the body and blood of Christ. To him, despised and ugly in the eyes of the world, and yet the most beautiful one, radiant with divine love, be all honour and glory, now and for ever.

Mary, Battered and Glorious Vessel

Feast of the Assumption
St Michael and All Angels, Chiswick
Revelation 11.19; 12.1–6, 10; 1 Corinthians 15.20–27; Luke
  1.39–56

THE REVD DR MELANIE MARSHALL

One of the iconic films of my childhood was *Indiana Jones and the Raiders of the Lost Ark*. It had everything – a rip-roaring plot, Nazis as the bad guys and a very young, good-looking Harrison Ford as the good guy. In the climactic scene our handsome hero, lashed to a post, looks on helpless as the villain throws open the lid of Ark of the Covenant – and with all the special effects that 1981 could muster, he and his fascist crew melt into human puddles by the power of God.

Had these godless Nazis read their Bibles instead of burning them they might have known better. Because the New Testament as well as the Old makes it very clear. You cannot look on God and live. Of course, God himself is pure spirit; he is invisible. But just to behold his glory, the light in which he dwells, is something that even angels can scarcely bear, and human beings not at all. Yet today the Church teaches that there, by God's very throne, is Mary. A mortal like us, and yet beholding God face to face. Unmelted.

And, even stranger, this is no anomaly. This place where Mary dwells is her true home. It's also our true home. But if European literature teaches us one thing, it's that no one reaches home without a journey.

Let's begin on Mount Sinai. There, God gives the tablets of the

Law, the Ten Commandments, to Moses who, his face shining with the reflection of the glory of God, brings the tablets to the people. The trouble is that at this point in Israel's history they have no home, no bookshelves. They are in a desert, wandering. Where are they going to put something as precious as the word of God itself?

Answer: an ark, a beautiful chest, built according to God's precise instructions. And in this chest, God's word is carried. Carried through the wilderness. Through wars. Captured by the enemy. Recovered. Hidden for safe-keeping. Quite a journey.

The Virgin Mary had quite a journey, too. She was hand-picked by God, formed precisely according to his will. Chosen to be the vessel who would carry God's Word – his Living Word, his Son. Mary went through the wilderness, too – she was a refugee from Herod's slaughter, when Jesus was a baby, and after his death goes into exile again. They say that any mother is only as happy as her least happy child. Imagine being the mother of that child. A child persecuted, reviled, killed. A sword pierces his mother's heart, as well.

A sword through the heart. Not so pretty. And yet we do take refuge sometimes in rather fluffy language. The perfect peace of knowing God. The joy of having Jesus in your heart. The surpassing gentleness of lovely Mary. Is that how it feels most days? Is that all that following Christ means for you? If it is, then you're doing it wrong. Look at Syria. Or Iraq, where the heads of Christian children are put on spikes. What about the things Christians across the world undergo day after day? The ridicule, the fight for the truth Christ has taught us. What about the struggle in every country to say that lives matter? Old lives, weak lives, ugly lives, criminal lives, poor lives, not just rich and strong and privileged ones. The Magnificat, the song that Mary sings in today's Gospel – it's a battle cry. Of those who are trying to bear Christ to the world, as Mary did. To make God's face and glory known. Hers is the cry of people everywhere who will not know peace in this lifetime.

Friends, Christ said it himself: I bring not peace, but a sword. Through the heart. And yet: Blessed are you when you are reviled and persecuted for my sake. Rejoice and be glad. For your reward is great in heaven.

What happens, then, to the Ark of the Covenant, after all its tribulations? It goes home. Solomon builds the Temple in Jerusalem, a home for the Ark at last. There the Ark is brought, and there it rests. Once a year, on the Jewish Day of Atonement, the High Priest would approach the Ark, and on it he would sprinkle blood, the blood of the atoning lamb of sacrifice. On a rather different Day of Atonement, Mary stood at the foot of the cross. There she was splattered with Christ's blood, spilt because the world is cruel and hateful. The Ark – this vulnerable vessel that bore God's Word with resilience, through tribulation and sorrow and fear and anguish and loss – is given the highest position, at the centre of the Temple. The Ark has earned that place of honour. And our Mother, Mary, assumed into the heaven of heavens, has earned her place of honour, too.

As for Solomon's Temple: destroyed. Razed to the ground by the Babylonians 25 centuries ago. Then rebuilt, and again destroyed, by the Romans, 20 centuries ago. The Ark of the Covenant and its tablets: gone. Not even Indiana Jones could find it now.

But we have a temple that cannot be destroyed. And that temple is Christ. Of course, people tried to destroy him. They still do. God has many, many enemies. Jesus says to these enemies: 'Destroy this temple, and in three days, I will raise it up' (John 2.19). He was talking of course about the temple of his own body. And because they tried and failed to kill Christ for good, because Christ has trampled down death by death; because he has put on imperishability, immortality – so have we. We have a home in him that can never be destroyed.

The mere mention of the Virgin Mary makes some of the more English kind of Christian call for loosened stays and smelling salts. But let's look at this sensibly. God has not done for Mary anything that he doesn't also will for us. Did he craft her in her mother's womb, designing her for a special purpose? He did. But so did he for all of us – *before I formed you in the womb I knew you*, says the Lord (Jer. 1.5). Did God keep Mary sinless? Yes. And St Paul says God *chose us in Christ before the foundation of the world* – chose us – *that we should be holy and blameless before him* (Eph. 1.4). God intends that holiness for all of us. In Mary it was fully realized.

How? Because she is full of grace. Yes, God gave her unique grace, because he gave her a unique role, to bear God in the flesh. But doesn't God give you grace? To bear your sleepless children and dementing parents and demanding jobs, and your needs and losses and hungers and those of the people you meet? Perhaps you feel God doesn't give you the grace you need. Have you asked him? *Cast all your anxiety on him, because he cares for you* (1 Peter 5.7). *Ask, and ye shall receive* (Matt. 7.7).

Finally God has taken Mary to himself: entire, body and soul, at the very moment of her death, to be united with Christ, whom she bore. To bear Christ to the world is to feel Christ's compassion, to look out on the world with Christ's eyes, on the weeping and hurting and wounding and bleeding of his brothers and sisters. Christ feels all the world's pain. And Mary feels Christ's pain. She does perfectly what every Christian strives to do. And what God wants at the end of that journey is for us, too, to be joined to Christ, as Mary is. To stand at his throne, and to know, at last, his peace.

God cannot show us himself in all his glory, not in this life. We would perish, like the Nazis in the film. And yet … Right at the foot of the throne of God, higher in honour than the Cherubim, incomparably more glorious than the Seraphim, is Mary. A mortal person like you and me. As we struggle on our journey – with doubt and indifference and error and neglect and weariness – she has finished her journey. And she waits at the journey's end, in the temple that is Christ. Her pain was Christ's pain, and now her hope is Christ's hope. The hope is this: that these battered vessels – we, who have tried, and failed, and tried again, and failed again, to carry God's Word faithfully through this world – that we too might, one day, come to rest in him.

Our Lady, Ark of the Covenant, pray for us.

Challenging Christians?

Trinity 10
Blackfriars, Oxford
Matthew 15.21–28

FR FERGUS KERR, OP

Canaanites are cast in a bad light in the Bible. Their gods are
Baal and Moloch, their goddesses Astarte and Ashera. They are
accused of practising fertility rites, sacrificing children and many
other abominations, on account of which 'the land itself vomiteth
out her inhabitants' (Lev. 18.25).

How much of this sinister reputation survived in New
Testament times it is difficult to tell. In Mark's version of the story
the Canaanite woman is described as a Greek, a Syrophoenician
by birth (Mark 7.26), identified by her non-Jewish language and
ethnicity rather than by her belonging to an idolatrous religion.
In Matthew's account, however, she is a Canaanite, who 'comes
out' from the vicinity of Tyre and Sidon, greeting Jesus as 'son of
David', taking it for granted that he has the power and authority
to liberate her demon-possessed daughter. According to the way
that Matthew tells this quite complex story, the woman believes
in his authority to help her more straightforwardly than Jesus
himself seems to do.

Jesus has just been hassled by Pharisees and scribes. He was
on the western shore of the Sea of Galilee, where people have
recognized him and brought all the sick they could find for him
to heal. The Pharisees and scribes have come up from Jerusalem
to accuse him of transgressing the traditions of the elders: his

disciples 'do not wash their hands when they eat' and suchlike. This leads to a lengthy argument. Growing trust among ordinary Galileans in Jesus, at least as a healer, is matched by increasing suspicions of his orthodoxy on the part of the religious leaders. They have discovered that his disciples flout the Mosaic legal traditions. Apparently failing to persuade them that what defiles a person is not eating with unwashed hands but what proceeds from the heart, Jesus suddenly turns away, as if in disgust, and travels as far north as he ever goes, to the border between his native Galilee and the Roman province of Syria. It is the clearest line, geographically, that he ever draws between his Jewish inheritance and the universal mission that is to come.

Geographical details in the Gospels often have symbolic significance and immense theological implications for the future. Since the woman 'came out' to meet Jesus it sounds as if, though in the neighbourhood of Tyre and Sidon, he did not go down to the Mediterranean coast where these great seaports were located. Tyre and Sidon of course still exist, in modern Lebanon. In New Testament times the inhabitants were mostly Gentiles, non-Israelites. The judgement on these two cities, Jesus has already predicted, would be severe, though less so than on the cities where most of his mighty works had been done – 'because they did not repent' (Matt. 11.20)! Symbolically, Tyre and Sidon evidently represent the wicked heathen world – though if he had done mighty works there 'they would have repented long ago in sackcloth and ashes' (Matt. 11.21). However, he may well have been able to see the Mediterranean in the distance: the sea that would take his message out to the Graeco-Roman world.

When the woman appeals to Jesus he does not reply. Angered by her screaming, his disciples interpret his silence as his wanting nothing to do with her. Seemingly, he agrees with them at first that his mission is uniquely to 'the lost sheep of the house of Israel'. Kneeling at his feet, however, the heathen woman persists. He repeats that he has nothing for the likes of her, putting it graphically, even quite brutally – he has no authority to give the bread of the children of Israel to 'dogs'.

It is not easy to take the sting out of what Jesus says here. Dogs are sometimes regarded as 'unclean' in the Bible, though never as explicitly as in Islamic tradition (hence the revulsion in the Middle East at the use of dogs by American soldiers to torture Iraqi prisoners at Abu Ghraib). After all, as he has said earlier, 'Do not give dogs what is holy, and do not throw your pearls before swine' (Matt. 7.6). That sounds clear enough.

'But it is fair', the woman retorts, unabashed, and certainly behaving with a panache that would have been rare for a woman in those days. Evidently she distinguishes between wild dogs and house dogs. Domestic dogs, she reminds Jesus, get the 'crumbs that fall from the table' – presumably the sodden lumps of pitta bread that functioned as spoons and napkins. These dogs, after all, belonged to the household. They were not like feral dogs scavenging outside in the garbage pits. In effect, they belonged in the house of the children of Israel. At her witty and even cheeky repartee Jesus' reluctance to engage with her suddenly dissolves – 'O woman, great is your faith! Be it done to you as you desire.' Perhaps he even dissolves into mirth.

It is certainly one of the very few funny stories in the Gospels. How much are we to make of it? Has Jesus just been teasing the woman, or is she testing him? Is this a turning point for him, his discovery, as he deals with her persistence, that his mission transcends the boundaries of Israel? Taking this episode, like so many others in the Gospels, as prophetic of what will unfold in due time, doesn't this exchange prefigure the venture of Christian faith into pagan territory? Doesn't this episode anticipate the vision vouchsafed to the apostle Paul at Troas, when he sees a man of Macedonia beseeching him to come over the Aegean Sea to Greece (Acts 16. 9) – as if the Christian mission to Europe was by invitation? Isn't this one of the episodes in the life of Jesus that inaugurate the universal mission of the Church?

Does the Canaanite woman represent the generations to come of people of pagan origins who would look to the Christian faith for liberation from idolatry and demonic possession? How many of them, in the event, were forcibly baptized at the behest of their rulers, or kept in the Church by the threat of excommunication and worse? Doesn't the structure of the conversation with the

Canaanite woman invite us to reflect on the possibilities – down the line – of mutual recognition between non-Christian religion and Christianity? Isn't this wonderful little story an invitation to reflect on the possibilities of liberation that pagans may hope to find in Christianity, and the necessity, if they are not to be disappointed, that we Christians discover possibilities in ourselves that call us beyond our inherited boundaries?

I Believe in Angels

Feast of St Michael and All Angels
St George's Church, Netherfield, Nottingham

The Revd Dr Robert Chapman

In 1979 four Swedes in unfeasibly tight spangled trousers said, 'I believe in angels', and several million people bought the record, sending it to number one in Austria, Belgium and Canada and even to number seven in the Zimbabwean singles chart! The sentiment Abba was expressing in the late 1970s has been repeated by the likes of Westlife and Robbie Williams in the karaoke and funeral anthem 'Angels'.

It appears that the world of pop would be infinitely duller without the allusion to angels.

The same is also true of major bookstores. While you'll struggle to find anything more orthodox than a Bible in the 'Religion and Spirituality' section, there are shelves full of such angelic classics as *The Angel Bible*, *Messages from Angels*, *How to Change Your World with Angels* and even, wait for it, *Angel Horses: Divine Messengers of Hope* by Linda Anderson.

It's no wonder that the preacher looks forward to this subject about as much as an evening in with all 256 pages of Ms Anderson's angelic equine tome. But the trouble is that as a church we can't really avoid the issue of angels and archangels. At every Eucharist, we declare our solidarity and participation in worship with angels and archangels and all the company of heaven, before joining their song: the Sanctus. At the end of the Mass at Netherfield we recall in the Angelus that the 'Angel of the Lord brought tidings to Mary'.

This scriptural declaration within the context of the Eucharist means that we simply can't dismiss the angelic as mere divine Postman Pats. Yes, as their Greek name suggests, they are messengers, but as Scripture shows they are so much more. Angels, according to the Psalmist (Ps. 148.2, 5) are a part of creation, yet they also have authority over the created order.

Jesus tells us in Matthew (Matt. 18.10) that angels have responsibility for children. Elsewhere they are protectors of God's people (Ps. 34.7) and participate in the judgements of God (Rev. 15–16). St Michael, whom we particularly remember today, has special authority according to the prophet Daniel (Dan. 10.13), Jude (Jude 9) and St John (Rev. 1.7). Angels are present at the resurrection (Matt. 28.2) as much as they were at the Christ's birth.

Angels crop up everywhere, whether it's scrapping in the middle of the road with Jacob or feeding a depressed Elijah. Yet, in spite of the accepted presence within the narrative of Scripture as those who reveal God's presence and declare his intervention in the world, shouldn't they still receive their P45 after the incarnation? After all, could God be any more present or intervene any more blatantly? Yet, even after the Incarnation God still hasn't rationalized them or created retirement opportunities for them.

So what is their point? I'm not sure they have to have a point that fits into our scheme. When we attempt to do this we not only run into all sorts of issues, scientific and philosophical, about the truth of them, but we diminish the mystery and also the vision of the world created by God. By trying to fit the angelic into a role, being or job description that we can label and file we commodify God's creation.

Angels reveal to us more than breaking news from the Almighty; they reveal a fullness to God's creation that takes us beyond the cave in which you dwell if you're Plato or the Shadowlands if you're C. S. Lewis. Plato once described humanity as living as though we dwelt in caves facing the wall, with the entrance to the cave behind us. The light from the entrance casts shadows of objects. Those objects we believe to be real because that is all we have seen. Yet beyond the mouth of the cave is the real world in its fullness. Of course we don't know we're staring at shadows on a wall, because we have never seen the outside, yet this day of all days opens the possibility of that world.

Today, as we grapple with the bewildering world of angels, we are shown a glimpse of the real world created by God in his inexhaustible, overflowing love. They may seem to be no more than winged silhouettes on our cave, but they give us a fuller framework for the universe. This real world, *kosmos*, exists within the life of God and we are caught up and welcomed into it.

Angels and archangels and all the company of heaven and those of us breaking bread uniting heaven and earth are part of *that* world. As we recall Michael, Raphael, Gabriel and all angels we are reminded of the God who comes to us, and keeps coming in love, so in the end this most heavenly of hopes becomes the most earthly of realities. It is recalling this that stops us from dreamingly gazing at white-winged cherubs and reminds us of God coming into a broken world.

Like Abba, I believe in angels, not because it makes sense in a world of objects and tangible beings, but only because I believe in a God who exceeds all my hopes, desires and Shadowlands.

Lord of the Harvest

Harvest Festival
Southwell Minster
Amos 8.4–7; Luke 16.1–13

THE REVD PROFESSOR MICHAEL NORTHCOTT

In Russia in 2010 much of the wheat harvest was destroyed by extreme heat. Vladimir Putin announced that Russia would not export any wheat that year. Russia has long resisted the idea that human fossil fuel use is connected with the warming climate of the planet, and taken the view that if climate change brings warmer weather, then Russian harvests will increase as more land becomes available in Siberia for food growing. But this has not been Russia's experience.

In Pakistan the same year the harvests were not gathered in when the floods came. And even if they had been they would have been wiped out when the store houses were flooded and ruined by rising flood waters of unprecedented extent and speed. Many hardly had the time to flee from their houses before the waters overflowed their doors and windows.

Wheat prices soared on wheat futures markets in London and New York because of the decline in Russia's wheat production. And in Mozambique there were food riots as the price of bread soared by 30 per cent, a price hike few people could afford.

Many blame these events on global warming. And yes, it is true that the hottest summer in Russia, the USA and in Japan – and the worst floods in Pakistan and Niger in a century – affected food production as well as seriously impacting on the poor. But what lies behind the food shortages still experienced by more than a billion people in the world is not our inability as a species to grow food. This year sees the third largest global wheat harvest on record.

It is not the weather but the preparedness of the masters of the universe – bankers, government and corporate leaders – to treat food like a tradeable commodity. Bill Clinton encouraged Haiti to abandon rice production and instead to grow cash crops to sell to the USA to pay off its foreign debts. But when Haiti was hit by a devastating hurricane in 2008 its already poor economy was in tatters, and it had no food surpluses of its own. Clinton now laments this: 'I have to live every day with the consequences of the lost capacity to produce a rice crop in Haiti to feed those people, because of what I did. … treating food like it was a colour television set.'

Economists have trained our leaders for more than a hundred years that food is like any other commodity and best managed by competitive international markets. And so we have encouraged the poorest countries in the world to give up growing staple crops like cassava, potatoes and rice and instead to plant cash crops: coffee in Vietnam, asparagus in Peru and cut flowers in Kenya. These crops drain water from their rivers and aquifers to pay the foreign debts corruptly lent by Western bankers to their often-corrupt governments so they can buy luxuries and weapons. When the globally warmed and strengthened storms or floods come, these countries have no stores of staple foods, and have reduced their ability to withstand natural disasters by selling their land and labour for TV sets or weapons. They are then at the mercy of those same bankers who now sell them wheat and rice at inflated prices.

The prophet Amos reflects on a similar situation in the land of Israel in the late Hebrew monarchy. He observes how the wealthy have trampled on the needy and ruined the poor of the land by creating artificial scarcities in wheat – storing it up in time and season, and then selling it short with the proportion smaller and the money greater. And hence – as in Haiti and Pakistan – as the debts mount up, and the storms rise, the poor have no food and their labour can be bought for the price of a pair of sandals.

We gather in this beautiful minster at the heart of a rich food-growing region to celebrate God's gift of a blessed earth and the harvest of good foods, represented in our midst by a nave draped with carrots and turnips grown by Frank Reynolds, a local farmer, on whose farm at Farnsfield next weekend will be held the Southwell ploughing match and show.

But even here in Britain we import 40 per cent of the food we eat from other nations, whose acreage we still live off long after the end of empire. Our civilization is in the midst of a bio-political crisis. Unless we learn again to live on the earth in a way that respects natural order and builds up rather than destroys the community of life with which we share it, we will find in years to come that the great financial centres of London and New York, Singapore and Shanghai and Tokyo will be inundated with rising seas and strengthening storm.

It was speculative trading that got us in Britain into our own political and financial crisis in 2008 when bankers grew rich and sleek on trading in derivatives based on debts to homeowners. And the reason is that the modern human economy lacks any sense of an objective moral order. The neglect of an objective moral order that the great medieval Doctor of the Church, Thomas Aquinas, called natural law is implicated in the continuing profligate use of coal and oil and gas even when we know that – as in the village of Hockerton just outside Southwell – we can derive our energy sustainably from the land around us without polluting the atmosphere and strengthening the storms that harm the poor.

Genesis 1 describes human beings as divinely appointed guardians, or vice-regents, of creation. Hence we have the capacity as creatures uniquely made in the image of God either to frustrate or to fulfil the destiny of creation. And what is that destiny? Well as we have been hearing – and as we celebrate today in our Harvest Festival – it is that all creatures join with us as we help make fruitful the earth in its abundant grace and goodness so that – as our harvest hymn declares – the hills with joy will ring, and the valleys thick with corn will sing, and join with us in a cosmic liturgy of thankfulness and praise to the Creator.

But what is the mystery of our nature as humans that so often makes us frustrate rather than fulfil this great and wondrous destiny? As Christ says in summing up the meaning of the parable of the Unjust Steward that is our Gospel today: you cannot serve God and wealth.

At the heart of the gospel is the message that the eternal law set into creation and set before God's people in the law of Moses has been fulfilled in the person and work of the Lord Jesus Christ. And looking down on us here from the nave roof is the risen Lord who promises us life when we worship him more than the things of this world. Peter Ball's wonderful sculpture of Christ is not a bloodied and crucified Christ – as so often depicted in Christian art since the Middle Ages. Instead it is an image of *Christus Rex*. Christ risen and ascended looks down on us in this image and reminds us that in his death our failure to be faithful with the goodness of the earth God has given us is forgiven, because Christ incarnate has borne the burden of our guilt and in his risen life has shown us again God's divine intention – to redeem all things and the creation itself from its bondage to our misuse.

It is this message of salvation through forgiveness that is also at the heart of our gospel story. The unjust steward has – like a greedy banker – misused the wealth of his master and is told he will get the sack. But before this happens, he decides to garner favour with those who owe his master money and so he calls each in and forgives a substantial portion of their debt. By putting friendship before money power, the unjust steward puts mercy before justice and so makes friends with his master's debtors. And the master also – when he hears of it – is pleased for he realizes that the steward has redeemed his honour *and* increased the honour of his master by forgiving his debtors. In the end he has served his master – and not money – and so he has found the way that leads to life.

When we put technological or money power above the health of field and leaf and atmosphere, we oppress the poor and we frustrate God's good purpose to redeem the land and humanity. But when we honour the eternal law set into the order of creation, when we forgive debts as our debts are forgiven us, we too will find that God replaces the spirit of fear that drives our need and greed for material security with love for God, for one another and for all creation.

Jesus Christ truly is Lord of the harvest – and he gives us more than enough for all our need, though not our greed. And when we, on our allotments, fields and gardens and in our homes, kitchens and markets, deepen our efforts to rebuild sustainable, locally based economies where food and energy are harvested in ways that respect the community ecology of this region – and the earth's atmosphere – then we are honouring the risen Christ who tells his disciples, and us, 'You cannot serve God and Mammon.'

The Feast of You and Me

Dedication Festival
Parish Church of St Margaret, Prestwich, Cheshire
I Kings 8.22–30; Hebrews 12.18–24; Matthew 21.12–16

THE REVD RICHARD STANTON

'Then was Jesus led up of the Spirit into the wilderness to be tempted of the devil' (Matt. 4.1). That was the text on which Bishop James Prince Lee preached when he came to consecrate this church on 18th March 1852. It was Lent. One of his hearers commented that 'the theme looked unpromising, but it was skilfully worked round to the more immediate occasion'. Maybe it's a warning to preachers to check the readings before accepting an invitation!

More promising was the text the Bishop used at the first service here on 26th October 1851: 'It is good for us to be here' (Matt. 17.4). Once a year, every church celebrates a Dedication Festival to remind ourselves of that fact, to give thanks to God for the gift of this consecrated place. But this is not just the feast of this building: it is a feast of you and me too, and it is more to do with the future than the past.

What are your memories of St Margaret's – whether you've been here for months or a lifetime? How does St Margaret's weave in and out of your life – bringing a child to the waters of the font to be made an inheritor of the Kingdom of heaven … standing nervously at the door as a bride (or even more nervously at the altar as a groom) on the edge of being knit mysteriously into one flesh … blinking back tears as the body of a parent, friend or child is borne out of church on its way to the silence of the grave to await the resurrection. And not just the grand events: what about the other moments of grace – the confirmations, the confessions, the silent prayers and whispered hopes and sinking regrets, the rare, unexpected stirrings of the deep love of God, the preaching and teaching which has deepened our hope in Jesus Christ who said that the hungry would be filled, and the meek would inherit the earth. And what about every Eucharist – the thousands of times a priest has stood at one of our altars and led the people in offering bread and wine, and receiving them back as Body and Blood, to remember the Lord's death until he comes.

But the church is not just the backdrop to those things; it is part of the story, part of our story. As Jacob said: 'Surely the Lord is in this place … this is none other than the house of God and the gate of heaven!' Today we give thanks not for a lifeless pile of stone and wood, but for an embassy of the Kingdom of God breaking into the world, into the lives of men and women in all times and places, in Jerusalem and Antioch and Rome and Prestwich … the Good News passing from person to person: 'Did you hear? He is risen, and has appeared to Simon!'

Our Old Testament lesson was the great prayer of Solomon when he dedicated the Temple in Jerusalem, the place where the covenant between God and his people Israel was kept and made present. This morning is riddled with mentions of the heavenly Jerusalem, the perfect city where the Lord dwells. He himself is the new Temple, and every church in the world is a sign of that Temple where Jesus, the great High Priest, is making atonement for his people and holding us in relationship with his Father.

Most of us cannot love in broad brushstrokes – we need to love particular things to help us to love more generally: a husband or wife, a beautiful garden, an adored grandchild, a church that is a sign here of the reality of the Church, the Household of Faith, throughout the world. 'We love the place, O God, wherein thine honour dwells: the joy of thine abode all earthly joy excels!'

Thine abode: not ours. It's especially easy when we love something to end up being possessive of it, to try to own it, but think of this morning's Gospel, 'My house will be called a house of prayer', says the Lord. His house, of which we are stewards. And when he says, 'My house' he means not just the Temple of Jerusalem, nor this church, but you and me. That's what he promised his friends as he said farewell in St John's Gospel: 'Those who love me will keep my word, and my Father will love them, and we will come to them and make our home with them' (John 14.23).

This church then is not just a building, but a construction site. We don't give out hard hats at the door and have big red triangles that say 'DANGER: GOD AT WORK', but perhaps we should. For to come to this place is to put yourself into the hands of that great Architect who first spun the heavens into life and set the stars on their course, the endlessly patient Craftsman who works away, building us into the image of Jesus Christ.

Through the sacraments we are being built up, transformed into citizens of that heavenly Jerusalem which the letter to the Hebrews speaks of, 'the city of the living God' (Heb. 12.22). And the architecture of Travis and Magnall, the painting of Graeme Willson, the embroidery of Judy Barry, the carving of Arthur Simpson and the silver of Leslie Durbin, though now they give their glory to God, in the end all these will pass away – but God's building, God's artwork, is you: and in the life of the resurrection that will never pass away.

This church gives us some clues to show us the kind of people our Master Builder is turning into it, if we let him. We have a font, because he desires to wash us and refresh us from his spring of living water welling up to eternal life, because he does not want us to be dry and thirsty and scraped out, but full of life and vigour. We have images of the saints, because it is not his will that we should be alone, but surrounded by friends waiting just out of sight: one family, together in the risen Lord. We have windows, because the Church must not be shut up on herself, but open to the world around her so that she may seek and serve God not just in here but out there – in those who are poor or disadvantaged or rejected, the troublesome people you cross the street to avoid. We have a doorway, so that all who need to may go out and come in and find pasture in him who is 'the door of the sheep'. We are surrounded in the roof by golden angels because we must always be telling the glory of God and playing a new song to him on the instruments of our lives. We have an aumbry to reserve the Blessed Sacrament, because he has promised that he will be with us always, to the end of the age.

Above all we have an altar, a place of offering and sacrifice, because this building work that God is doing with us will hurt and be costly and sometimes we will feel that we cannot go on with it because it is too painful – the church is shrinking, nobody cares, I don't see the point. But the altar is for us not only the cross, on which the Lamb was slain to take away the sins of the world, but also the empty tomb – the place from which a living glory came forth – and the table of the Last Supper, where Jesus 'gives himself' to feed his people with their daily bread.

We will look like this, in the end. What a building this is going to be, this building which is you and me and everyone who wants to be part of it! 'In Christ the whole structure is joined together and grows into a holy temple in the Lord,' said St Paul (Eph. 2.21).

But that can only happen if we cooperate with him, because unlike the stones of this building, which had no choice about being hauled around and laid one on top of the other, that is not God's way with the living stones of his Church. With Mary we must say: 'Yes: be it unto me according to thy will.'

That means being truly a 'Church Family', a body of brothers and sisters in baptism who care for one another, tend each other's needs and speak in love to one another. That means really being a eucharistic community, the Lord's family, who wouldn't dream of being without the Lord's own Supper on the Lord's day. That means being a family that seeks Jesus in word and sacrament, 'seven whole days, not one in seven'. That means being a family that looks outward and seeks to draw in other people using our imagination, courage and love, not settling for anything less than always hoping, praying and working for growth. That means being a family that doesn't exclude, doesn't divide into factions or cynical groups, but rejoices in its richness, young and old together, all supporting one another as stone on top of stone. In and through this we will discover that we are the Lord's 'house of prayer', Jesus our High Priest praying in us and with us and taking our fragile offerings up into his own perfect offering to his Father.

Thanks be to God for 163 years of St Margaret's Church, the beauty of holiness. Thanks be to God for those who built it, adorned it and loved it and have made it a sign in Prestwich of God's love and faithfulness: may light perpetual shine upon them. Thanks be to God for all St Margaret's means to us and all he has given us here.

And now let us go on in the Lord – it will be hard; we will need all the faith and hope and love we can muster; but still with St Paul we 'press on towards the goal for the prize of the heavenly call of God in Christ Jesus' (Phil. 3.14). In season and out of season, for better for worse, for richer for poorer, 'we are God's servants, working together; you are God's field, God's building' (1 Cor. 3.9).

Holy Fear, Holy Play

St Mary the Less, Cambridge
2 Kings 5.1–3; 7–15c; 2 Timothy 2.8–15; Luke 17.11–19

THE VERY REVD DR FRANCES WARD

It is good to read from Psalm 111, set for today, that the fear of the Lord is the beginning of wisdom. Good to reflect upon fear, and its relation to wisdom. I find myself beginning, like poor old Michael Finnegan, again, and again, and again in wisdom. Frustratingly, it doesn't seem to accumulate year on year like some healthy bank account accruing interest. I can't look back and say – Well, I'm wiser than I was three years ago; in five years' time I will be even wiser than I am now. Oh, why doesn't it work like that? And then the fear of the Lord. Why such a negative emotion as the beginning of wisdom? The easy option is to explain it away as 'respect'. Perhaps better, 'awe'. But somehow that's not good enough. Respect for the Lord is the beginning of wisdom? I don't think so.

Naaman was well acquainted with fear. Other people's, on the whole. A commander; a mighty warrior. Used to big decisions, leading from the front; shrewd in judgement; a clear strategic talent. Able to see the wood in spite of the trees – and the trees in the wood. A mind shaped by purpose, focused, executive. And then he is faced with leprosy. To begin with, mild symptoms – a slight tingling in his fingers; but then the skin dying, starting to flake off. The slow and increasing debilitation. The loss of everything that makes him great. This is an increasingly desperate man, who doesn't know where to turn, full of rage born of unaccustomed fear.

It's deceptively simple, the request of the prophet from Israel. So deceptive that Naaman responds in anger. What's wrong with his own rivers? Isn't he important enough that the prophet will come out to him? But he takes the advice of his servants, and does as he is told. His fear humbles him, and brings him to something more profound, to the recognition of God: 'Now I know that there is no God in all the earth except in Israel.' So often it begins here for us too, the turn to God out of desperation. Fear can leave us with nowhere else to go, that blinding fear that takes us and closes down our options until there's nothing we can do, but begin to listen, to accept that we are dependent.

The fear of nothingness, of death, of waste. And so we shield ourselves with purpose. We get caught up in functionality. Striving to reach – and prove that we have reached – measurable targets. Setting goals and strategies; following processes. We find a purpose in life to block out fear. We measure ourselves by success. Then the greatest fear we face is the fear of failure. Which is easy to manage, for we work harder; we make sure we succeed. It's a pattern very familiar in today's society, beset as it is with that instrumental rationality we see everywhere. This enables us to avoid the fear of having nothing to do, of having no purpose. It functions very effectively to shut away the deeper questions of the purpose of our lives. Or even that purpose might not be what we are about.

It is, after all, the fear of the Lord that is the beginning of wisdom. Not the fear of leprosy, or failure, or any other one of innumerable fears that can beset us. And it's an extremely important distinction. Yes, when we reach the end of our tether, and are exhausted by fear, then often we turn to the Lord. But when we do, it's a very different sort of fear that we encounter.

Romano Guardini, a twentieth-century Roman Catholic theo-logian, wrote:

The soul must learn to abandon, at least in prayer, the restlessness of purposeful activity; it must learn to waste time for the sake of God, and to be prepared for the sacred game with sayings and thoughts and gestures, without always immediately asking 'why?' and 'wherefore?' It must learn not to be continually yearning to do something, to attack something, to accomplish something useful, but to play the divinely ordained game of the liturgy in liberty and beauty and holy joy before God.[21]

Herbert McCabe has said something very similar: that prayer is about wasting time in God. Both are encouraging us to be purposeless, to challenge the need to be useful, functional, instrumental.

Fear can bring us to the Lord; the fear of the Lord seems to encourage us to play. We are a society very much in danger of losing the art of play. Donald Winnicott wrote powerfully of the importance of play in a child's life. To develop as human beings, and grow into adult life, they need the opportunity to play; to take risks emotionally and physically, to learn to cope with danger, to find resources within. And for adults, Winnicott argued, the playfulness continues in art and culture. Here are goods that are not about purpose. No picture painted for a purpose can be called art – art is simply an expression of liberty and beauty and holy joy before God. Adults play when they go to a play; they play when they paint, or stand in awe and delight before a glorious piece of embroidery, or read a Donne sonnet. The play of the child, in which he is lost, is continued as the adult loses herself in the contemplation of beauty. For then we touch truth. Or the truth touches us. There is a profound relationship between truth and beauty. Guardini said, in no uncertain terms, that truth is the soul of beauty. Beauty is not beauty if it doesn't in some way witness to truth. When it becomes a slave to functionality, or profit, or purpose, beauty is lost before it is found.

If a society beset by instrumental rationality has no time to play, it sees no sense either in worship. Why are we here this morning? We come simply to be in the presence of God, to be encountered by the truth. As Naaman was, when he washed himself seven times. We are here to waste time for the sake of God, says Guardini, to be prepared for the sacred game with sayings and thoughts and gestures. The liturgy is full of sayings and thoughts and gestures – of profound significance, just as a small child, playing, is caught up in the significance of the rules and actions of the game. Play is for its own sake. The worship of God – the liturgy – is for its own sake, or rather, for God's sake.

As we worship, we are face to face with that which is more to be feared than anything else that can be imagined. We enter a realm that is not ours. A realm not curtailed by the petty purposes and mundane routines of our lives, but a realm of God, of delight that transforms us and reminds us that our souls find their rest in God's eternal glory. The moment of judgement of our lives is anticipated each time we enter the realm of worship. Each time we approach God we open ourselves to the most profound fear. For here we are stripped and pruned, heated and refined, distilled and purified. The sins we recognize are taken out of our hands, and we find ourselves aware of what we have not begun to comprehend. We face the Lord in fear.

The liturgy holds us through that encounter: the grace-filled liturgy that brings us to repentance and assures us of absolution; that consoles and feeds us with word and sacrament; that challenges us out of our narcissism and into service and love of neighbour. We come into the real presence of Christ, we receive him in bread and wine. We come knowing that no cheap grace is here, but that the fear of the Lord is the beginning of wisdom.

Was it Thomas à Kempis who told us to dare to begin? And then to begin and begin again? And we do start again and again, coming back to the touchstone of the truth of our lives as we encounter God, here, in church, in the purposelessness of the liturgy. We become disciples, and disciplined, in the divine play which shapes us to learn that the presence of God is to be feared beyond anything else in life. For it renders us ends in God's eyes, not means in the eyes of others.

What a thing to show the world! How much it needs to see and understand: that we are not governed by means, but are ends – that each of us is made for God's sake, not for a purpose that needs to be fulfilled, measured, understood. You and I – we are children of God, here to play, with Eternal Wisdom; forming all things, who was delighted every day, playing before him at all times, playing in the world. Today, as we celebrate the Mass, we enter into a different time and space – a time and space that belongs not to us, but to the Lord. We come with fear and trembling, knowing that in word, in bread and wine, we are encountered and brought back to our first and only end, which is to glorify God.

And from here we must go out into the world to see and encounter others with the eyes of God. To resist that insidious trend to make this colleague an end to my means, to turn that situation to my advantage, regardless of the cost to others. We must challenge the dehumanizing utilitarianism around us. We must look for wisdom, and value it, and seek to be wise in our judgement. Knowing that our wisdom is not ours, but finds its source here, in the encounter with the truth of God experienced in worship, that begins in fear. This is a holy fear that reminds us that we are his children. That it is in playfulness that we discover all that we are given. In holy fear we rejoice and begin to be wise.

Remembering Well

Remembrance Day
St Mary's, Battersea
Amos 5.18–24; Matthew 25.1–13 (AV)

THE REVD DR PHILIP KRINKS

At 7.20 p.m. on 14th November 1940 bombs began falling on the city of Coventry. The main targets were the city's weapons factories and industrial infrastructure. At around 8 p.m. an incendiary bomb hit Coventry Cathedral and it was set on fire. Volunteer fire-fighters were on duty that night in the cathedral and they put out the first fire, but more fires followed. By the time the all-clear sounded on the morning of 15th November, two-thirds of Coventry's buildings were damaged, one-third of the factories were completely destroyed – and the cathedral was a burnt-out ruin. About 30,000 civilians took to surrounding country or to air-raid shelters and were saved. Sadly, more than 500 lives were lost.

One month later the RAF launched its first incendiary-intensive raid of the war, on the city of Mannheim.

And ten days after that the Provost of Coventry Cathedral, Dick Howard, made a remarkable Christmas Day radio broadcast on the BBC. Speaking from the ruins of the burnt-out cathedral, he said that after the war Britain should work with those who had been enemies 'to build a kinder, more Christ-like world'.

Then he gave this intention physical form. He had the words 'Father Forgive' inscribed on the walls of the ruined chancel. Two charred beams that had fallen in the shape of a cross were placed on an altar of rubble. Three medieval nails that had been blasted free of the ancient structure were formed into a cross. This Cross of Nails became the symbol of reconciliation between Coventry, Dresden, Berlin and Kiel in the late 1940s. Today the Community of the Cross of Nails is a movement of 150 peace and reconciliation workers across the world.

One thing that is striking about Dick Howard's words and actions is how little time passed between the raid and the commitment he made to forgiveness and reconciliation: about six weeks. He might have been reading today's Gospel: what must be done should not be delayed. Put oil into the lamp of your faith now, when you can, for you never know when you will need it. There is no time to delay. Now is the time to prepare for and to bring in the Kingdom: to turn towards truth, towards healing and towards hope.

For Dick Howard in Coventry, remembrance was necessary. So it is for us today, as we remember the sacrifices made in war, especially those made in the last hundred years. Remembrance is necessary for three reasons. First, remembering is required for truth, for honouring the reality of the past. Secondly, remembering is required for healing and reconciliation. Memory can be 'the bridge between adversaries' as well as a gulf that separates them. Thus says the theologian Miroslav Volf in *The End of Memory*, which discusses Volf's own experiences of violence in communist Yugoslavia. Thirdly, remembering is necessary for hope, for learning how to seek a better future, learning about what it is that we hope for.

No remembering is easy. Howard's was not. Ours is not. No part of it is easy. First, honouring the reality of the past is not easy: for the past is traumatic, when we consider our own experiences, and those of our communities, and indeed those of the communities we counted as our enemies. Secondly, healing and reconciliation are not easy, because the human instinct is to hate and seek revenge, when we feel ourselves wronged. Thirdly, learning is not easy, because it is so easy to learn only superficially, to entertain false hopes, to hope for a fantasy. When we think of false hopes, we might think of the 'fantasy peace' of endless compromise, where it is never necessary to stand up for what is right – and we might think the last hundred years in Europe show us that that is indeed a fantasy.

We might also think of the words of Amos. He tells us that we may think we desire the day of the Lord; but what we often in fact desire is a fantasy about that day. If that's what we do, then seeking salvation from a lion we are liable to run unexpectedly into a bear. Seeking the shelter of a house, we will put our hand on the wall and a serpent may bite us. We only seek the day of the Lord truly, Amos says, if we are willing to pray with him, 'let judgement run down as waters and righteousness as a mighty stream'.

Remembering well can only be done in faith. Our faith not only calls us to the work of remembering, it also gives us the resources for it. By grace we are able to remember the events of the past in the light of the whole of salvation history: God's good creation, human falling short, slavery, exodus, Christ's incarnation, teaching, crucifixion, resurrection, Ascension, Pentecost. By grace we are able to place our own experiences and those of our communities in the context of our own lives of faith. By grace we can find the courage to face reality, through our trust in God's good purposes for us and all his world.

So let me suggest three prayers we can make this morning: that we may be strengthened not to delay in filling the lamps of our lives with the oil of faith; that we may not delay in doing the difficult work of remembering; and that God may bring in his Kingdom of peace, of freedom from pain and death, and of the reconciling love which is able to overcome all hatred and division.

Higher than the Angels

Baptism
Jesus College Chapel, Cambridge
Revelation 12.7–12; Luke 1.26–38

THE REVD DR JOHN HUGHES

What does baptism have to do with angels? Is the selection of this day, to link in with the angelic Feast of Michaelmas, with those readings and hymns, just a continuation of an Italian joke upon the surname Angelici: naming not only the first child, Gabriel here, but also the second one, Raphael, whose baptism we celebrate today, after archangels. (I hope you don't continue to four, by the way!) Well, perhaps it is, but I think we can find a deeper meaning here, for thinking about angels can tell us more about the meaning of baptism, both in the ways that angels are like us and the ways they are different from us.

In popular piety, children are often associated with angels. I am sure you've seen those rose-tinted pictures of them praying together? Now we may baulk at this, but I think there is a truth here that is hinted at in various parts of the Scriptures. Angels, throughout the Scriptures, are part of the heavenly court, attending directly on the presence of God, basking in his light, waiting simply to do his will, ascending and descending upon the Son of Man. And this we believe is truly our ultimate destiny as well: we were created to worship and love and enjoy God for ever and our worship on earth seeks to be a foretaste of that joy. In this sense, angels show us something of our destiny, our birth-right, our inheritance, given to us in baptism. Raphael, you were created to enjoy God for ever and this is the inheritance you will receive in just a moment through these waters! And if angels show us something of our destiny, so too do children, as Christ indicates in Matthew 18.3, 10: 'Unless you become like a little child, you shall not enter the kingdom of Heaven ... truly I tell you their angels in heaven behold the face of my father.' Angels and children are closely associated by Christ and both are linked with entry into the coming Kingdom. Children (on a good day at least) are free of all that adult complexity and guile and world-weariness. Like angels they are a sign of that total dependence, that simplicity and humility, that contemplation of the face of God, which is the Kingdom of God. But if angels are a sign to us of the contemplation which is the goal of the Christian life, that is not all! They do other, active things as well, be it Gabriel bringing good news or Michael fighting against the forces of darkness and evil in the world, which is something else that we will pray for you, Raphael, when we anoint you. And of course, appropriately, given what your mother does, Raphael is the archangel of healing. Fighting against evil, bringing healing and sharing good news is a good outline of some of the things a Christian is called to do, the vocation, Raphael, that you are given in your baptism. So angels can remind us of contemplation and the vocation to serve, two aspects of the Christian life which begin for Raphael today in baptism.

Yet in another important way, angels are not like us, and this is a difference that won't ever be overcome. Angels don't have material bodies like us, which means their existence is not as social or temporal as ours. Angels don't need other angels and they don't need time as it were. Which is also why they don't need or cannot enjoy the benefits of sacraments. We need other people and time to work out our salvation. You will have the whole of your life and the support of all these people and others, Raphael, to work out the fruits of your baptism. This is why God become incarnate not as an angel, but as a human being, Jesus, raising our humanity above the ranks of angels into the life of God himself. Even the angels, we heard in our Revelation reading, have conquered not by their own power, but 'by the blood of the Lamb'. Baptism is not just about the angelic innocence of children, or the vocation to become like angels, it is about God washing away all the sin of the world through the death and resurrection of Jesus Christ and incorporating us into his holy Church, his ark of salvation. Angels, after all, cannot be baptized: this privilege is for us alone! This, then, is what we are about to do for you, Raphael!

Divine Athletes

Confirmation
Lincoln College Chapel, Oxford
1 Peter 3.13–end; John 14.15–21

The Right Revd Dr Stephen Platten

In the same way that we expect John Humphrys to introduce the *Today* programme each morning, in the mid-twentieth century there was only one serious commentator for the Oxford and Cambridge boat race, one John Snagge. Snagge was a professional, indeed even a little pompous, but he too made his gaffes. Most famous of these was at a most exciting moment, when the boats were neck and neck, Snagge astutely commented: 'They're so close I can't see who is ahead – it's either Oxford or Cambridge.' *Private Eye* details such gaffes weekly in its 'Colemanballs' column. Last week it was Rio Ferdinand on Radio Five Live who remarkably commented: 'Gary Neville *was* captain, and now Ryan Giggs has taken on the mantelpiece.'

It's very easy to make such gaffes when a microphone is thrust before you. Truisms just escape one's mouth. Here's another: all sport is good clean fun. Before we sign up to that, let me transport you across Europe to Berlin. Travel east-west along the main Heerstrasse, the spine road that crosses Berlin, and to your left, halfway along, rises the great Olympic stadium. It is one of the surviving monuments of Nazi Fascist architecture designed by Albert Speer, the architect to the Third Reich. It still breathes a certain style. Here, in 1936, at the Olympics, Adolf Hitler, Chancellor or Führer of Germany, refused to present Jesse

Owens, a black American athlete, with his gold medal.

Because sport, Hitler knew, is serious business. Part of the Nazi vision was the golden-haired athletic Arian man – man at his so-called best, partaking of a new transformed existence. Sport was part of an all-encompassing, but perverted, ideal for life. Hitler's vision was not new. It harked back to a fresher and more wholesome ideal, shared by the ancient Greeks, whereby one's development as a human and integration as a citizen could be prepared by physical training and athleticism. The Greek vision of the academy, a place to train body, mind and spirit for the common life of the city-state, shaped the different cultures of late antiquity.

And the baptism and confirmation we are celebrating today takes us back similarly to the earliest Christian vision, also springing out of late antiquity. For Christian baptism and confirmation, initiation that is, was fashioned in the image of the early Olympics. Lent began with Ash Wednesday as the start of 40 days taxing training. Those who opted for baptism, the catechumens as they were known, set out on a spell of intense preparation. St Paul of course uses the image of the athlete in his letters.

Easter Sunday was the culmination of this remarkable programme of training. In Holy Week, you entered the final depths of darkness. At the vigil on Easter Eve these athletes would be put through their paces in baptism. Taken down a few steps, near the entrance to the church, into something like a stone coffin, they would die and be raised in Christ.

We have become very dainty about baptism over these two millennia. There is a great deal of lace and incised marble. But not so in the early days. Go to Sandringham parish church, and outside in the churchyard you will see a font just like a coffin, looking now rather like an empty flowerpot. Brought back by an earlier monarch it would have seen many baptisms some 1,800 years ago somewhere at the eastern end of the Mediterranean. Baptism was indeed a serious business. All of you will know of the leaning tower of Pisa, a detached cathedral bell tower. Less famous, but equally stunning is the dome-like baptistery next to it, guarding the west door of the cathedral. Nothing could be too striking for the great sacrament of baptism.

And this is what Ashley, Will and George are either embarking upon or completing this evening. In that sense those who say that sport is a serious business have got it right. The races we run in baptism and confirmation *are* the gateway to a transformed existence. In that extract from John 14 which we have just heard, the Christian way is set in a similar context of disciplined preparation that opens us to transformation:

> If you love me, you will keep my commandments ... They who have my commandments and keep them are those who love me; and those who love me will be loved by my Father, and I will love them and reveal myself to them.

The pattern that is unfolded here is the diametric opposite of Hitler's ugly dream based on hatred, holocaust and hubris. The life of God in Jesus is fashioned only by love and grace; grace, that is, God's free gift to us in Jesus. Looking out over the Umbrian plain from Assisi in April 1945, politician and future Prime Minister Harold Macmillan reflected: 'Hitler has lasted just 12 years – with all his power of evil, his strength, his boasting. St Francis did not seem to have much power, but here in this lovely place one realizes the immense strength and permanence of goodness.'

Francis recaptured Christ's vision rooted in love; his *poverellos*, his little poor friars, transformed Europe even in Francis' own lifetime. That transformation is offered in Ashley, Will and George this evening. It is a transformation our world desperately needs. These three are the sort of athletes whose strength is a spiritual mystery, not external muscle: who can, with God's grace, run his race, and effect that transformation.

God's Designer Label

Confirmation
Holy Rood Church, Carnoustie, Scotland

The Right Revd Dr Nigel Peyton

I was in George Street, Edinburgh last week. It's full of designer-label stores and quite trendy. Some of them I just don't understand, like Hollister, which is dark inside and full of mirrors and plasma screens, colourful back-lighting and music. You can't read the price-tags, it's like shopping in a night club. Maybe that's the point.

Perhaps some of you today are wearing designer labels, or aspiring to having them. Designer labels indicate that we aspire to be fashionable and are possibly well off. Or that we just like to wear nice stuff and, well, maybe that we are a bit vain. Who isn't? Or a bit stupid, because we could have got something similar but much cheaper at Primark. The whole point of designer labels is that they are worn on the outside and are visible – and in the famous words of the cosmetics television adverts they remind us that 'we're worth it'.

The latest variation on our obsession with appearance is of course the 'selfie' photo, taken on a mobile phone, which proves where we were and who with. So perhaps we'll take one right now to record that our candidates were baptized and confirmed by their bishop in this church today. [At this point the Bishop produced his iPhone and some 'selfies' were taken.]

The Christian baptism and confirmation that we celebrate today signify becoming ever more part of the worldwide Christian family. The whole occasion is filled with visible signs and actions, 'labels' if you like, to help us understand what is going on. We have the water in the font and the sign of the cross, the Christian badge – some of the ladies may have cross and chain around their neck, and the church building is of course full of Christian symbols. We have godparents and sponsors and promises, we have prayers and the laying on of hands and anointing with chrism oil, candles and certificates. And we share the bread and wine and blessings of Holy Communion.

Baptism and confirmation are door-opening moments, steps on the lifelong journey of faith. They are not like MMR jabs, an inoculation against the ups and downs of life. But as older members of this congregation will tell you if you ask them (which you should), the Christian faith has certainly sustained them over many years. For candidates and their families this is a new beginning, a big moment, a 'yes to God' moment. It is a time to celebrate parenthood, youngsters and family life, and growing up in the world. It is a time to recognize the dreams and aspirations of young people heading out in life with their talents and enthusiasms, and their understandable anxieties.

Being a teenager is full of very human contradictions. Teenagers demonstrate touching kindness and sheer bad temper; they have strong opinions, making amazing efforts to solve complex problems one moment, and yet can also be switched off and not bothered. The young are care-free and confident and anxious and doubt-ridden, all at the same time, moody and unpredictable, with the sheer excitement of all of life ahead of them.

We are not simply going through the motions today. Because today's baptism and confirmation celebration is all about a very different sort of designer label. This label from our designer never goes out of fashion. It is unrepeatable, indelible and indestructible; it is unending and can never be stolen from you; it is invisible and costs nothing.

As sacraments of the Church, baptism and confirmation are all about God's grace and blessing: they are to be worn on the inside of a person. They are about the interior life, about the real you, the secret you that God nevertheless sees and loves and cares deeply about – whatever happens to you in life, and for ever. Because God knows 'you're worth it'.

As our Bible readings today remind us: God's spirit of truth 'abides with you' (John 14.17) which means God takes up residence inside a person, God moves in. Likewise, St Paul took the view that 'all who are led by the spirit of God are children of God' (Rom. 8.14). In other words, we become members of God's family – we move in with God.

Baptism and confirmation are about believing without knowing it all for now. The congregation today are not simply spectators, but fellow sponsors, supporters and disciples. The Christian life is a long journey and every day we pray that God may be in us, and be made known through us, and in the life of this church and our diocese: this year's chapter in the Acts of the Apostles.

Each time we come to church and receive the bread and wine of Holy Communion, or a blessing, we are nourished in our daily Christian life, both the outward public expression and the private interior parts. And especially when our outside and our inside don't match very well – you know, when we put on a cheerful exterior which hides the sad or anxious inside of ourselves. At the heart of our liturgy are some beautiful words that sum up both the prayer and the promise in what we are doing today: 'In Christ your Son, our life and yours are brought together in a wonderful exchange. He made his home among us so that we might for ever dwell in you.'

This is our prayer for the candidates today – after all, you can take a 'selfie' with the Bishop, but you don't need to take a 'selfie' with God, because God has already moved into your life, for ever.

The Abundant Economy

Wedding Eucharist
Southwell Minster
Isaiah 62.1–5; Romans 12.1–2, 9–15; John 15.9–12 (AV)

THE REVD CANON PROFESSOR SIMON OLIVER

Arabella and James, you come to the altar to be blessed and strengthened by God's grace, binding yourselves in the sacrament of marriage and being fed by the sacrament of the Eucharist. Our Scripture readings speak of the character of marriage: union, nurture, care, mutual protection and sacrifice, all bound together in the love of God made known in Christ. The proclamation of Isaiah is set in the midst of new hope following the destruction of the Jerusalem Temple and the exile in Babylon. God's people had been driven from their promised land in ignominy and violence. But they will no longer be forsaken and the land will not be desolate. As they return home to Jerusalem, God's gift of the land to his people will be renewed and they will receive a new identity. 'Thou shalt be called Hephzibah', we are told. This is the name of the wife of the King of Judah, Hezekiah, and it means 'my delight is in her', a term that is often used of God's relation to Israel, who is God's delight. The root meaning of Hephzibah evokes tender protection and guardianship. God will protect his people as a bridegroom protects his bride. As the people receive again God's abundant gift of land, the prophet likens the relationship between the people and the land to marriage. They will not own it but be united to it as spouses are united with each other in marriage. Their identity and blessing will be bound to the land as they nourish and care for it. God's people have travelled from desolation to marriage, from emptiness to the abundance of God's blessing. This brings joy: 'as the bridegroom rejoiceth over the bride, so shall thy God rejoice over thee.' God gives the land to his people and his people to the land. God gives bride to bridegroom and bridegroom to bride.

That relationship of nurture, protection and guardianship will require the spirit of sacrifice about which St Paul writes to the Romans: 'present your bodies as a living sacrifice ... And be not conformed to this world: but be ye transformed by the renewing of your mind.' When we speak of sacrifice today, we tend to think in terms of giving something up. I might sacrifice my goods, even my life, for the sake of something else, and this means giving up something valuable and important. To receive something in return for one's sacrifice would somehow compromise its selfless character. So sacrifice concerns a lack of something, an abandonment, a grief at the loss. In fact, this is an important characteristic of the world to which St Paul tells us we must not be conformed. It is our world that speaks of lack before it speaks of abundance. The science of economics, which dominates our political culture, begins with the assumption that the world is characterized by a lack of resources in the face of limitless and anarchic human desire. We are somehow lacking in resources and must sustain human flourishing and relationships – even marriages – against the odds.

But this is not quite how the Bible envisions sacrifice. To offer sacrifice is to dedicate something to a particular and holy purpose. Such sacrifices do not occur within an economy of lack, but within an economy of God's abundant providential blessing. To offer our bodies as a living sacrifice is precisely to live, to live in the expectation of a response, a return blessing, without anticipating what that response might be.

Arabella and James are not married within the world's economy of lack, but within the abundant economy of God's love. Their marriage will flourish not against the odds with only the limited human resources of good will and sentiment, but in the faith and hope that, offering themselves as a living sacrifice, they will *live* to receive from God the abundant blessings which bring fruitfulness and flourishing. The character of the sacrifice of your marriage is described by St Paul: cleave to what is good; be kindly affectioned one to another; in honour, prefer one another; be patient, instant in prayer, generous to the saints and given to hospitality. Rejoice together; weep together. In sacrificing yourselves in this way, you live, you live to wait patiently for the Lord and the glory of his gracious love.

The form of that gracious love is shown to us in Jesus. He says to his disciples, 'As the Father hath loved me, so have I loved you: continue in my love.' Christ comes to God's people with a specific commandment: 'That ye love one another, as I have loved you.' How has Christ loved us? Christ's love is exemplified in his own sacrifice, the offering of his life on the cross to reconcile the world to God. But Christ does not offer this sacrifice within an economy of impoverished lack, but in the obedient faith that, beyond the dereliction and total defeat of the cross, the Father's eternal and abundant love will make all things new in the Spirit in ways that we can barely imagine. So the crucified Christ is raised to new life on the third day and opens the gates of heaven. What looked like a sacrifice of death reveals an eternal living sacrifice that God invites us to share: the Son's eternal return gift of himself to the Father in the Holy Spirit.

Jesus commands that we love one another as he loves us in the context of his teaching that he is the true vine into which we, as branches, must be grafted. This passage from St John's Gospel repeats many times that we are to abide in Christ and abide in his love. The image is deeply intimate. In turn, Christ's joy is to remain in us that our joy might be full. This is not a love that we are to imitate or copy at a distance. Human love does not mimic divine love. Human love finds itself within the love of God, in the grafting of our bodies and souls into Christ. Arabella and James graft themselves and their marriage into Christ today as they receive into their bodies his eucharistic body and blood. They will abide in that sacrificial love, giving themselves to each other and their marriage to the Church as signs of the abundant economy of God's grace.

Within a culture that sees in the world poverty and lack, and that regards sacrifice as something occasionally necessary but somewhat regrettable, the divine economy of abundant sacrificial love will seem alien and strange. Marriages will be entered into with a sneaking sense that they flourish somewhat against the odds, courtesy of good will and dogged determination. The gracious love into which Arabella and James graft their marriage, the love *in* which they will abide, provides the abundant grace which means that you can faithfully rejoice and weep together, that you can delight in each other and forgive each other. Your marriage is not simply of your own making, but is and always will be God's gracious gift to you. Having made of your marriage a living sacrifice, you can wait patiently for the Lord, for the blessings he will bestow in response. There begins the reciprocal love in which you will abide for the rest of your days. So nurture each other, protect each other, care tenderly for each other, delight in each other as God delights in his people and as Christ claims the Church as his bride. Through the sacrament to which you submit yourselves today, you will become a gracious blessing to each other and to the world, being God's gift to us all.

Are You Real?

Ordination of Deacons
Ely Cathedral
John 13.1–15

The Revd Anna Matthews

'Are you real?' This is a question I suspect most clerics get asked at one time or another. It happens in supermarkets, in pubs, on public transport, on the street when you're just minding your own business – and, my favourite time, when I was representing the Church of England at a wedding fair. This well-intentioned attempt to encourage people to consider getting married in church saw myself and a colleague in collars and cassocks manning the Church of England's stall. Which, to our amusement and the evident dismay of the person in charge, was sandwiched between something called 'boot-camp brides', to help you get in shape for the big day, and a company offering pole-dancing lessons for hen nights. There's incarnational ministry for you. It took a lot of convincing people that we were real, and not just actors brought in from central casting.

'Are you real?' Usually when asked it's because you don't quite fit the stereotype people carry about in their heads of what an ordained person looks like – some monstrous amalgam of Father Ted, the Vicar of Dibley, and the benignly ineffectual clerics of Agatha Christie novels. But it's a good question for all Christians to ask themselves, and especially the ordained, who can very easily become parodies or adopt personas, rather than living as the real human beings God calls. And it's as real human beings that Max and Jon come to ordination tonight. They're the same people as they were yesterday; the same people that many of you here have loved and supported and shaped down the years. But they will leave this cathedral tonight changed for ever.

'Are you real?' is a particularly important question for a deacon to answer. This is because the Church has become somewhat forgetful of what a deacon's ministry is, and those outside the Church have probably never known. The temptation is to define yourself in terms of what you're not: that you're not a priest; that you're not quite fully qualified; that the L plates still haven't come off. When I was ordained deacon my training incumbent said to me, 'You're not really much use to me this year.' There were probably all sorts of reasons why that was true, but the fact that I was a deacon and not a priest shouldn't have been one of them. As we see in the service tonight, the office of deacon is a valuable ministry in its own right, and if we know how to receive it, a great gift to the Church and the world. Jon and Max are called to share in the servant ministry of Christ. They are ordained, as the Bishop said at the start of the service, 'so that the people of God may be better equipped to make Christ known'. And as St Paul writes, the variety of gifts given to the Church is 'to equip the saints for the work of ministry'.

So Max and Jon, your role is to help us relearn what a deacon is, and so to help us all share more fully in the ministry that Christ has entrusted to his Church. In a short while the Bishop will set out for you an impossible job description, which will require you to be heralds of the Kingdom, proclaimers of the gospel, agents of God's purposes of love. It will tell you to have a particular concern for the poor, the weak, the sick, the lonely, the oppressed and the powerless. And it will ask you to be for us icons of Christ, who came not to be served but to serve.

And it's right, and I'm glad, that it's an impossible job description. Because if it wasn't you might make the very serious mistake of thinking that you could do it on your own. It struck me with disturbing clarity when I was a curate that you can get quite far in the Church of England if you work hard, are reasonably bright, and don't annoy the bishop too much. You are both bright, gifted, charming and committed, so you'll need to be alert to this risk. And it is a risk, because it encourages you to depend on yourselves instead of on God. Don't. We are in grave danger in the Church of England of professionalizing the ordained ministry to such an extent that we start to believe it's all about competencies that can be assessed, rather than about character, which is imputed by God and grows through our hidden life of prayer.

For those of you here to support Jon and Max tonight, the first thing they will need from you is prayer. They can't do this on their own. So, pray that they may grow daily in the image of Christ the servant king, and be given grace to live out the promises they make today. And the second thing they will need from you is courage.

The calling laid on Max and Jon as deacons in the Church of God is to be lived out primarily among you. It's given so that you, the people of God among whom they are to serve, may be better equipped to make Christ known. Receiving a deacon should come with a health warning. Their ministry of prayer, of proclamation, of searching out the vulnerable and marginalized, and of ministering to those in need doesn't let you off the hook because you've got someone else there to do it for you. Quite the reverse. Having a deacon will ask you to become more faithful in prayer for the world and its needs, braver and more confident in proclaiming the gospel, and more compassionate in reaching out into the forgotten corners of the parish. If they are to live out their vocations properly, they will make you more servant-hearted too. And that needs courage, because while we can talk quite piously about seeking and serving Christ in the generalized poor and outcast, we're not always so happy with the idea of seeking and serving him in the particular person of the swaying, dishevelled drunk who disrupts the end of Evening Prayer, or in the lonely widow whom dementia has robbed of her memories and sense of fun. But the Christ who came to serve, of whom Max and Jon are to be icons, will ask you to go with him and for him into the brokenness of the world, to minister his healing and peace. And then he will ask you to come back, bearing the people and their needs on your hearts, and offering them to him in prayer, and most especially in your prayer at the Eucharist.

This is the ministry deacons are sent to enable. And this twofold action is what saves deacons from being oddly dressed social workers. You are to be signs to us, or walking sacraments, to borrow Austin Farrer's phrase, of Christ, our crucified and risen Lord. Don't let your actions leave people in the belief that Jesus was simply a good man and moral teacher whose example we might follow. Rather, live in such a way that the only possible explanation for your life and the way you serve others is that Christ is risen from the dead. Be alongside those the world has no time for because you have glimpsed eternity, and have all the time given by Christ's victory over death. Search out those who are lost, or lonely, or empty, and show them, by the way Christ lives in you, the more excellent way of the gospel. Feed the hungry, but don't ever leave them starving for the word of God and the bread of life.

An extraordinary responsibility is laid on you both tonight. And to be icons for us of Christ the servant, you will need first to let him serve you. Remember what Jesus says to Peter in the Gospel: 'unless I wash you, you have no share with me'. You will only be able to serve others with Christ's love to the extent that you have let him serve you. Pride, fear, insecurity, cynicism – there's a whole host of reasons to react like Peter and to say hotly 'you will never wash my feet'. But as you let Christ serve you, as you allow him to tend your wounds, to cleanse your sin, to raise your humanity to his, you will discover more truly who you are. You can do it without letting Christ serve you. Some do, because it's less costly that way. But if you do that you will be a fake. Your call is to be real – to let Christ's life be visible in you, so you can call us to a fuller sharing in that life. My training incumbent said something much more helpful than his comment that I wasn't much use as I was leaving for my ordination retreat after a year as a deacon in the parish. He said this: 'At the ordination the bishop will ask you, "will you, will you, will you?" Remember that one day another will ask you "did you, did you, did you?"' Max and Jon, remember that, and whose minister you are. But remember too that the God who calls you is faithful, and he will do this.

Overlapping Gifts

First Mass of Fr John Hughes
St Michael and All Angels, Exeter
Acts 8.14–17; John 14.15–31

CATHERINE PICKSTOCK

It must have seemed shocking for the very first Christians to hear that there was a gift that they had not yet received; surely, they must have thought, they had already received everything there was to receive, things so high that they could scarcely be imagined? They had been baptized in the name of God incarnate, and by this means they understood that their sins had been obliterated and that they now participated in the divine life itself. This must have seemed tantamount to having received everything and more than everything. What further gift could there be? Yet now there were rumours of a second baptism, in the Holy Spirit.

We seem to be confronted here with a question of superfluity. A second gift is an extra, and the supplementing of God's sovereign action with intercession is yet another. But here a more fundamental question arises about the need for an initial gift at all, since a gift is always of itself a kind of unnecessary extra. In the same way, the giver of a gift is a member of a kind of redundant supporting cast in human life both over and above and alongside the utilitarian structures of mutual co-operation and commercial exchange. One might say that when a gift arrives, it 'overlaps' our everyday life of the fulfilment of needs and satisfaction of desires. It is present with existing relations, and yet it overflows, laps over them. Similarly, the giver of a gift overlaps, and so reorientates our ordinary human interactions. And a person who intercedes on our behalf in order that we might be given a gift overlaps with prayer, and reorientates the runnels of human speech.

Acts 8 abounds with such curious superfluous overlappings. No sooner has Samaria been supplemented with the word of God than it has to welcome the strangers Peter and John speaking of the second gift, the descent of the Spirit, which takes the visible form of an overlapping – a hovering of imparted power and beneficence over peoples' heads.

Why then is there a need for a gift, and for givers and pleaders that there might be a gift? Why the need for this overlapping? Why is there a need in the New Testament for a second gift?

Perhaps the Gospel reading provides a clue. Here we find Jesus asking the hearers of his word to keep his word: this tells us that we cannot receive a gift once and for all. Even if a gift is the greatest gift imaginable, we cease to receive it if we abuse it. In fact, the greater the gift, the more we can never have done with receiving it, for we have never fully explored its resources. When we receive a gift, we need to ask for a second gift, which is the gift of being able to keep faith with the nature of the gift. It might seem greedy, if one has received a gift, straightaway to ask for another one; and yet in the case of a real gift, this is actually a part of gratitude. The most real gift is of something from somebody who possesses something one does not have. Just for this reason, receiving this sort of gift cannot be accomplished once and for all. And if one is grateful for such a gift, one will want to receive more of it.

But there is a further point: Jesus asks that people keep his word, but he does not say what this word is, any more than he defines what he means by speaking in the name of the Father, or the disciples speaking in his own name.

Here again we find instances of bizarre overlappings. The word that Jesus speaks will substitute for him when he is gone; yet this word is not his own, for Jesus has borrowed the word from the Father, and he overlaps with the Father in speaking it. Jesus and the Father seem to overlap one another in speaking, and both are further overlapped by the Spirit who is to come in place of the absent Christ.

Since we do not know what the gift is, so in trying to interpret this gift, we are open to receiving it in new ways. Here we discover a clue to the balance in Acts between intercession and grace: the apostles have to engage in the process that the mediaeval English poet William Langland described as 'fyndinge', a kind of active exploration which is also a receptivity. Just because the initial gift is an unnecessary but beneficent overshadowing of our lives, a superfluity, it is not a finished product or commodity. To be a gift, it must issue forth as gift-beyond-gift. It has endlessly to repeat itself. The very meaning of the first gift is therefore that there will be a second gift which stands for an infinity of gifts to come. And the meaning of the apparently superfluous accompaniment of our lives by giving persons and intercessors on our behalf is that there will always be more such persons mediating within our lives.

What is asked for must always overtake, as more than has been anticipated, in such a way that we receive inwardly and outwardly more treasure than we expect, and are touched and affected by infinitely more others than were ever sought out. It is perhaps for this reason that Jesus says that he does not give 'as the world gives'. Does this mean that the world gives badly, or in a niggardly fashion? Surely not, for the world gives in abundance all that we know that there is to give. So if the divine gift exceeds even this overabundance, we must say that it overtakes even plenitude as the gift and promise of the unimaginable and the hidden unsealed source of the world's providing.

For every real gift, then, there has to be a second gift. One might say, every gift has a Pentecostal structure. This is most of all true of the supreme gift of the Son of God and his sacrifice. After the event of the incarnation, and still as part of this event, there has to be the second event of the coming of the Spirit. Although this happened for a first time, it goes on happening.

However, the message of the Gospel reading is not entirely one of joyful super-abounding. Jesus' departure is a return to the Father, a reassurance of their mutual overlap. And, at the same time, it will allow the arrival of the new more intimate overlapping of ourselves on earth by the Holy Spirit.

We can understand the priesthood into which Father John

has just been inducted in terms of the true character of hyper-abundant overlapping. All Christians, but priests most especially, are in the position of the apostles: their work is to try to achieve an active receiving of the arrival of the second gift, which will allow us to be faithful to the words of Jesus and will also show us what those words are, and, indeed, will add to those words, and will thereby show that these additions were always already there.

In both our texts, we see a prominence accorded to distances, and to comings and goings; there is a gap between Christians in different places; a gap between those who have received the gift of the Holy Spirit, and those who have not; an interval between Jesus and the Father; there will be a gap between Jesus and the disciples after he has ascended; a distinction to be made between Jesus and the Holy Spirit – Jesus' departure allows the Spirit's arrival.

In every case, the interval between the giver and the recipient means that the gift is not a form of this-worldly dominance. We depend on God, but also he hands something over to us and allows us to appropriate it freely for ourselves. This is why Jesus had to go away in order not to go away; this is why he had to make way for the third person of the Trinity, in order to fulfil his nature as the Word.

Father John is now stepping into this logic. He is not being called to preserve unchanged a message that we have already comprehended. He is rather being called to explore this message, and to receive it again in so radical a fashion that he becomes contemporary with the apostles and with Christ himself.

Finally, as an apostle, it is his special work to try to ensure that his congregation also can become in its own fashion priests and apostles. He is called to do this through an active strategy of prayer and liturgy and an attentive life of pastoral practice. It will be his strange task to act as the necessary, because superfluous, person who constantly overlaps with the life of the people in his parish through co-working, sympathetic counsel and intercessory prayer. He is himself to be a giver, and a beseecher on behalf of his recipients for further gifts. These gifts themselves can only be disclosures of that eternal over-flowing which is the life of the Trinity and the eternal overlappings of Father, Son and Holy

Spirit. It will be Father John's work further to entangle the world in this web of abundance. At the same time, it will be his work to guard his flock against the snares of the false shadowing of this world by its usurping ruler.

As John's own dissertation concluded, a generous labour and an intercessory contemplation come together, as Langland's 'fyndinge', in the liturgical life that has at its centre the act of the Eucharist over which the priest alone can preside. What happens in the Eucharist seems to be so ordinary: the presentation of the most basic fruits of human labour; the eating and drinking of the most unremarkable sources of sustenance and good cheer. What is extraordinary is that so much should be made of this ordinary, that it should be exalted into the extra special which every day accompanies and overlaps our usual lives. But that is because, in performing this extraordinary and ordinary act, the priest is both repeating and anticipating the divine-human acts that sum up and include all possible acts – those of God and of creation, now, for our deification, fused together.

Soon, then, Father John will perform all that it is possible to perform. And yet the mystery is that we, as the congregation, will not be able to see this unless we realize this plenitudinous symbolic act in deeds of everyday charity, forgiveness and mercy. Here once again we see the mystery of the gift and of multiple personality, the mystery of the overlap. The all, the plenitude of fulfilment, the act of acts is only complete as offering us the infinite. This can never be finished in our usual, mortal sense. God, in the Eucharist, gives us all there is to give, but to receive this, we must go on receiving it in an openness of response which is deed as well as contemplation.

So to be ordained priest is to be inserted into a long chain in time, and it is to commence the salvation of the world all over again, as it were from its outset. For at every Eucharist, the promise of realized salvation is overtaken by a surprising superabundance of grace, in such a way that it is always as if, here, for the first time, the gift has been given, the world has been healed, and it is possible once more to set forth, not alone but always positively shadowed and surrounded by a visible and invisible company of countless others.

Repeating Ourselves

Requiem of Canon Robert Baily
St John the Evangelist, Manthorpe
Psalm 95 (BCP)

The Revd James Robinson

We have heard how beloved Bob was as father, grandfather, great-grandfather and friend. He was also a consummate priest, who may in his latter years have swapped his stipend for a pension, but who never retired. And so, although in recent times he has been a parishioner in need, he never ceased to be a colleague also, with much to teach me. Visiting him, in hospital not long before he died, I asked him how he was. And his only lament was the fact that because he could no longer read he was unable to say the daily offices of Morning and Evening Prayer. 'O come on Bob', I said, 'you must have some of it off by heart. What about the Venite?' (the name given to Psalm 95, which begins the office of Morning Prayer). And sure enough he proceeded to proclaim the words of that psalm with perfect recall. And the sight of a 95-year-old priest, on his death bed, proclaiming those words of faith moved me greatly. Indeed, I had never heard that psalm spoken with such deep resonance and power: and I will never be able to think of it in the same way again.

'O Come,' it begins, 'let us sing unto the Lord, let us heartily rejoice in the strength of our salvation.' He spoke its words at a glacial pace, with eyes tightly closed, voice gravelly, perfectly conveying the unstoppable strength of which the Psalmist sings. The weakness of his aged body was transfigured – and I do not use the word lightly – by the faith that was channelling through him.

It is a priest's lot to repeat oneself. Words of confession and absolution; of gospel proclamation; of intercession; of creedal belief and the promise of peace; of consecration and of blessing. This is our work, our liturgy, and it is performed in all sorts of situations, most demonstrably at the altar – but certainly not only there. Such repetition is also an essential part of the priesthood of all believers. We all relive year by year, as part of the Christian community, the annual cycle of failure and forgiveness, of feast and fast, of death and rebirth. Above all we repeat words. 'Our Father'; 'Lord have mercy'; 'Glory be to Thee'; 'Alleluia Amen'.

To the uninitiated cynic this may appear to achieve nothing more than the needless confinement of the individual in an institutionalized circle of self-denial and reproach; the crushing of the human spirit, illustrated nicely by the reference in the Venite's tenth verse to the lost wanderings of the Jews in the desert.

In one sense, of course the life of prayer is the principal *work* of the Christian; but it is not performed begrudgingly or aimlessly. It is the free response of the heart to the reality of the resurrection by one who has, on some level, encountered the risen Christ. It is, as such, the very way of our liberation.

Our round of worship and devotion echoes the eternal praise of the angels, and lifts us momentarily beyond the confines of time as we walk this earth. Our disciplines of service and prayer, of love manifested horizontally and vertically after our Lord's command, prepare us to join those angels on a more permanent basis.

The words we use may be the same but we never pray the same prayer twice, for we are never the same. They transform us, grow us in the likeness of God, so that day by day, word by word, breath by breath, we are made 'perfect, as our Heavenly Father is perfect'. This is our human destiny, to find our completion in the divine. Christ lowered himself to our estate: in Christ, we are raised to his.

And so, when I said that I had never heard anyone proclaim the Venite as Bob did before he died, it is also true that Bob had never proclaimed it in such a way before either. What had gone before had prepared him for that moment, which in turn prepared him for what lay ahead. The Venite is, remember, traditionally recited at the morning office. As Bob dwelt in the fading twilight of this life he was able to herald the dawning of the life to come.

And so, may he be liberated from his burdens; may he be reunited with those who have gone before him; may he be granted rest where the light of our Lord's face may shine upon him; may the Kingdom of heaven be his! And 'let us heartily rejoice in the strength of our salvation', that *we* may follow his many good examples until we meet again.

Further Reading

On Radical Orthodoxy

Radical Orthodoxy: A New Theology, ed. John Milbank, Catherine Pickstock and Graham Ward, London: Routledge, 1998.

The Radical Orthodoxy Reader, ed. John Milbank and Simon Oliver, London: Routledge, 2009.

Selected Books by Contributors

Anthony Baker
Diagonal Advance: Perfection in Christian Theology, Eugene, OR: Wipf and Stock, 2011.

Jeffrey P. Bishop
The Anticipatory Corpse: Medicine, Power, and the Care of the Dying, South Bend, IN: University of Notre Dame Press, 2011.

Ian Boxall
Discovering Matthew: Content, Interpretation, Reception, London: SPCK, 2014.

Patmos in the Reception History of the Apocalypse, Oxford Theology and Religion Monograph series, Oxford: Oxford University Press, 2013.

Matthew Bullimore
Graced Life: The Writings of John Hughes (1979–2014), (ed.), London: SCM Press, 2016.

Andrew Davison
Blessing, London: Canterbury Press, 2014.

The Love of Wisdom: An Introduction to Philosophy for Theologians, London: SCM Press, 2013.

Why Sacraments? London: SPCK, 2013.

For the Parish: A Critique of Fresh Expressions, with Alison Milbank, London: SCM Press, 2010.

Imaginative Apologetics: Theology, Philosophy and the Catholic Tradition, (ed.), London: SCM Press, 2011.

Peter Groves
Grace, London: Canterbury Press, 2012.

Stanley Hauerwas
The Work of Theology, Grand Rapids, MI: Eerdmans, 2015.

Hannah's Child: A Theological Memoir, Grand Rapids, MI: Eerdmans, 2012.

The Peaceable Kingdom: A Primer in Christian Ethics, South Bend, IL: University of Notre Dame Press, 1983.

John Inge
A Christian Theology of Place, Farnham: Ashgate, 2003.

Living in Love: In Conversation with the No. 1 Ladies Detective Agency, Newmarket: Inspire, 2007.

Fergus Kerr
Thomas Aquinas: A Very Short Introduction, Oxford: Oxford University Press, 2009.

Twentieth-Century Catholic Theologians: From Neoscholasticism to Nuptial Mysticism, Oxford: Blackwell Publishers, 2007.

Contemplating Aquinas: On the Varieties of Interpretation, London: SCM Press, 2007.

Alison Milbank

Theology and Literature after Postmodernity, ed. Peter Hampson, Zoe Lehmann Imfeld and Alison Milbank, London: Bloomsbury, T & T Clark, 2015.

For the Parish: A Critique of Fresh Expressions, with Andrew Davison, London: SCM Press, 2010.

Chesterton and Tolkien as Theologians: The Fantasy of the Real, London: T & T Clark, 2007.

John Milbank

The Politics of Virtue: Postliberalism and the Human Future, with Adrian Pabst, London: Rowman and Littlefield, 2016.

Beyond Secular Order: The Representation of Being and the Representation of the People, Oxford: Wiley-Blackwell, 2014.

Being Reconciled: Ontology and Pardon, London: Routledge, 2003.

Jeremy Morris

The Church in the Modern Age, London: I.B. Tauris, 2007, also published as D*as Christentum im 20. Jahrhundert. Kirche zwischen Politik und Gesellschaft*, Stuttgart: Kreuz Verlag, 2008.

An Acceptable Sacrifice? Homosexuality and the Church, ed., with D. Dormor, London: SPCK, 2007.

F. D. Maurice and the Crisis of Christian Authority, Oxford: Oxford University Press, 2005.

David Moss

The Cambridge Companion to Hans Urs von Balthasar, ed., with Edward T. Oakes, Cambridge: Cambridge University Press, 2004.

Edmund Newey
Children of God: The Child as Source of Theological Anthropology,
London: Routledge, 2012.

Michael Northcott
Place, Ecology and the Sacred, London: Bloomsbury, 2015.

A Political Theology of Climate Change, Grand Rapids, MI:
Eerdmans, 2013.

*Cuttle Fish, Clones and Cluster Bombs: Preaching Politics and
Ecology*, London: DLT, 2010.

Simon Oliver
Creation: A Guide for the Perplexed, London: Bloomsbury, 2017.

Philosophy, God and Motion, London: Routledge, 2005.

Faithful Reading: New Essays in Honour of Fergus Kerr, O.P.,
with Karen Kilby, Tom O'Loughlin and Simon Oliver, London:
Bloomsbury, 2012.

Nigel Peyton
Managing Clergy Lives: Obedience, Sacrifice, Intimacy, with
Caroline Gatrell, London: Bloomsbury, 2013.

Catherine Pickstock
Repetition and Identity: The Literary Agenda, Oxford: Oxford
University Press, 2013.

Truth in Aquinas, with John Milbank, London: Routledge, 2001.

After Writing: On The Liturgical Consummation of Philosophy,
Oxford: Blackwell, 1997.

Stephen Platten
Vocation: Singing the Lord's Song in a Strange Land, London:
SPCK, 2007.

Rebuilding Jerusalem: The Church's Hold on Hearts and Minds, London: SPCK, 2007.

Dreaming Spires? Cathedrals in a New Age, London: SPCK, 2006.

Jenn Strawbridge
The Pauline Effect: The Use of the Pauline Epistles by Early Christian Writers, Berlin: de Gruyter, 2015.

Frances Ward
Why Rousseau was Wrong: Christianity and the Secular Soul, London: Bloomsbury, 2013.

Lifelong Learning: Theological Education and Supervision, London: SCM Press, 2011.

Graham Ward
How the Light Gets In: Ethical Life I, Oxford: Oxford University Press, 2016.

Unbelievable: Why We Believe and Why We Don't, London: I. B. Tauris, 2014.

Cultural Transformation and Religious Practice, Cambridge: Cambridge University Press, 2010.

Endnotes

1 Joseph Ratzinger, 2011, *Dogma and Preaching: Applying Christian Doctrine to Daily Life*, San Francisco: Ignatius Press, p. 16.

2 Cyril of Jerusalem, *Catechetical Lectures* 15.1, in 1996, *Nicene and Post-Nicene Fathers*, ed. Philip Schaff, Series II, 14 vols, Edinburgh: T & T Clark, VII, 103.

3 Henri de Lubac, 2000 [1959], *Medieval Exegesis, The Four Senses of Scripture*, trans. E. M. Maceriowski, London: A. and C. Black, p. 217.

4 Andrew of Caesarea, 2011, *Commentary on the Apocalypse*, trans. E. S. Constantinou, Washington, DC: Catholic University of America Press, p. 219.

5 John Donne, 2000 [1633], *La Corona 2, Annunciation*, in *The Major Works*, ed. John Carey, Oxford: Oxford University Press, p. 171.

6 Julian of Norwich, 2015, *Revelations of Divine Love*, trans. Barry Windeatt, Oxford: Oxford University Press, p. 126.

7 *Revelations*, p. 120.

8 Robert Jensen, 1997, *Systematic Theology 1: The Triune God*, New York and Oxford: Oxford University Press, p. 14.

9 Lancelot Andrewes, 1841, *Ninety-Six Sermons*, London: J. H. Parker, p. 204.

10 Thomas Pestel, 1906, 'Behold the great Creator makes', *The*

English Hymnal, London: Oxford University Press, p. 18.

11 Barry Unsworth, 2007, *The Ruby in Her Navel*, New York: Norton, p. 30.

12 Eugene Rogers Jnr, 2013, *Aquinas and the Supreme Court: Narratives of Jews, Gentiles and Gender*, Oxford: Wiley-Blackwell, p. 258.

13 Gregory Nazianzus, Orations 1, 5, in 1886–1900, *Nicene and Post-Nicene Fathers*, Series II, 14 vols., London: T&T Clark, VII, 203.

14 Quoted in Martin Smith, 2004, A Season for the Spirit: Readings for the Days of Lent, New York: Church Publishing, p. 179.

15 Marguerite Shuster, 1997, 'The Preaching of the Resurrection of Christ in Augustine, Luther, Barth, and Thielicke', in *The Resurrection*, ed. Stephen Davis, Daniel Kendall, and Gerald O'Collins, Oxford: OUP. The references to Augustine are taken from this essay.

16 Joseph Ratzinger, 2004 [1968], *Introduction to Christianity*, trans. J. R. Foster, San Francisco: Ignatius Press, pp. 305–6.

17 Carl Schmitt, 1985, *Political Theology: Four Chapters on the Concept of Sovereignty*, trans. George Schwab, Chicago: Chicago University Press, p. 36.

18 Schmitt, *Political Theology*, p. 46.

19 Michel Quoist, 1963, *Prayers of Life*, London: Rowan and Littlefield, pp. 13–15.

20 St John Chrysostom, Homily 46 in 2004, *Homilies on St John*, trans. Philip Schaff, *Nicene and Post-Nicene Fathers*, Series I, 14 vols, Peabody MA: Hendrickson, XIV, p. 166.

21 Romano Guardini, 1997 [1935], *The Spirit of the Liturgy*, trans. Ada Lane, New York: Crossroad Publishing, pp. 71–2.